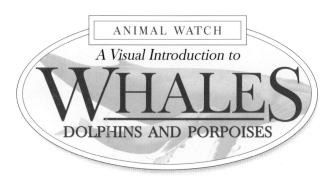

ANIMAL WATCH

A Visual Introduction to

WHALES

DOLPHINS AND PORPOISES

NO LONGER PROPERTY OF
KING COUNTY LIBRARY SYSTEM

Whales: A Visual Introduction to Whales, Dolphins and Porpoises
Copyright © 1998 AND Cartographic Publishers Ltd
http://www.and.nl
Created and Packaged by Firecrest Books Ltd. in association
with AND Cartographic Publishers Ltd.

All rights reserved. No part of this book may be reproduced or
utilized in any form or by any means, electronic or mechanical,
including photocopying, recording, or by any information
storage or retrieval systems, without permission in writing
from the publisher. For information contact:

Checkmark Books
An imprint of Facts On File, Inc.
11 Penn Plaza
New York NY 10001

Library of Congress Cataloging-in-Publication Data
Stonehouse, Bernard.
Whales: a visual introduction to whales/Bernard Stonehouse
illustrated by Martin Camm
p.cm. – (Animal watch)
Includes index.
Summary: In text and pictures, describes the various
kinds of whales, their life cycles, and the
best locations for humans to see them.
ISBN 0-8160-3922-4 (alk. paper)
1. Cetacea - Juvenile literature. 2. Whale watching - juvenile
literature. [1. Whales. 2. Whale watching.] I. Title.
II. Series: Stonehouse, Bernard. Animal Watch.
QL737.C4S762 1998
599.5-dc21   98-25058

Checkmark Books are available at special discounts when
purchased in bulk quantities for businesses, associations,
institutions or sales promotions. Please call our Special Sales
Department in New York at (212) 967-8800 or (800) 322-8755.

You can find Facts On File on the World Wide Web at
http://www.factsonfile.com

Illustration previous page: a bowhead
whale and southern right whale with calf

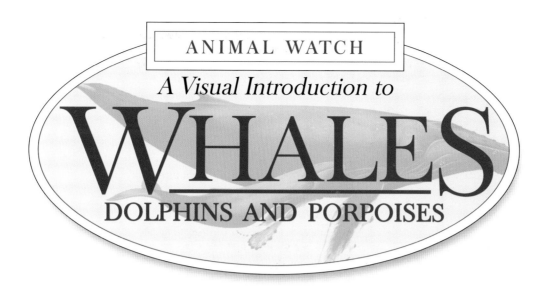

ANIMAL WATCH

A Visual Introduction to

WHALES

DOLPHINS AND PORPOISES

Bernard Stonehouse

Illustrated by Martin Camm

Checkmark Books™

An imprint of Facts On File, Inc.

KING COUNTY LIBRARY SYSTEM, WA

PICTURE CREDITS

AND Map Graphics
Mapping on pages 8-9

BBC Natural History Unit Picture Library
Pages 12-13 tl, tc; 17 tc, rc; 19 tr, b; 23 tc; 29 rc; 34 cb; 39 cb;
40-41 lb, rt, rc, rb; 44 lt, lb

Bernard Stonehouse
Page 15 rc, rb, c

Frank Lane Picture Agency
Pages 10 lb; 15 ct; 21 rc; 29 ct; 33 rc; 40-41 cb; 44-45 lc, rt, rb

International Fund for Animal Welfare
Page 37 ct

Natural History Photographic Agency
Pages 17 rb; 40 tl; 43 lt

Oxford Scientific Films
Pages 12-13 lb, rb; 26-27 c; 30-31 lb, rb; 36 lc

Robert Harding
Page 25 rt

Woodfall Wild Images
Pages 22-23 lb, rc; 24-25 tr, rb; 26-27 ct, c; 34-35 ct, rc; 37 rc;
38-39 lc, rb; 42-43 cr

WorldSat
All satellite mapping

l=left, r=right, c=center, t=top, b=below

Art and editorial direction by **Peter Sackett**

Edited by **Norman Barrett**

Designed by **Paul Richards, Designers & Partners**

Picture research by **Lis Sackett**

Color separation by **Job Color, Italy**

Printed by **Casterman, Belgium**

CONTENTS

Whale watching 8

Whales, dolphins and porpoises 10

Whales at home 12

Humpback whales 14

Bowhead and right whales 16

Blue whales 18

The smaller rorquals 20

Gray whales 22

Narwhals and belugas 24

Killer whales 26

Sperm whales 28

Bottlenose whales 30

Pilot whales 32

Dolphins 34

Porpoises 36

Cetaceans ashore 38

Cetaceans and man 40

Whales blowing 42

Glossary 44

Index 46

WATER TEMPERATURES

Surface temperatures of tropical and subtropical seas are usually above 77°F (25°C), and may reach 86°F (30°C) or more in summer. Always they are cooler below the surface. Even tropical seas may have temperatures as low as 39–41°F (4–5°C) close to the bottom. Temperate seas range from 50°F (10°C) or less in winter to 68°F (20°C) or more in summer. In polar seas surface waters are usually close to freezing point. Temperatures may fall as low as 29°F (-1.8°C) when ice is about, and seldom rise above 39°F (4°C) even in summer.

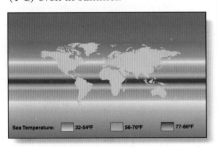

Sea Temperature: ☐ 32-54°F ☐ 56-76°F ☐ 77-86°F

Whales, dolphins and porpoises, like nearly all other mammals, have body temperatures close to 102°F (39°C). They are warmer even than the warmest seas, and much warmer than cold seas, so they tend to lose heat to the sea all the time. However, they are well protected by blubber (p. 13), and seem to prefer living in cool or cold seas, which often contain more food than warm seas.

WHALE WATCHING

WHERE, HOW AND WHEN TO GO

Where can we go to see whales, dolphins and porpoises in the wild? There are whales in every sea, but some are much easier to find than others. This map shows us where to look.

WHALES, DOLPHINS and porpoises swim in all the world's seas and oceans. Dolphins and porpoises also live in rivers and lakes. Not all kinds of whales are easy to see. Some live far from land and keep away from ships. We see them only when they have died and been washed ashore. Others are much easier to see, because they swim into shallow water or make regular journeys along coastlines at particular times of the year. We know where to look for them, and the best times of year for spotting them. Often you can see them quite easily from small boats, or even from beaches or cliff-tops.

THIS MAP SHOWS SOME OF THE BEST PLACES FOR SEEING WHALES.

Several species produce their calves in warm seas, where they hardly feed at all. Then they migrate to colder seas for several months to fatten up.

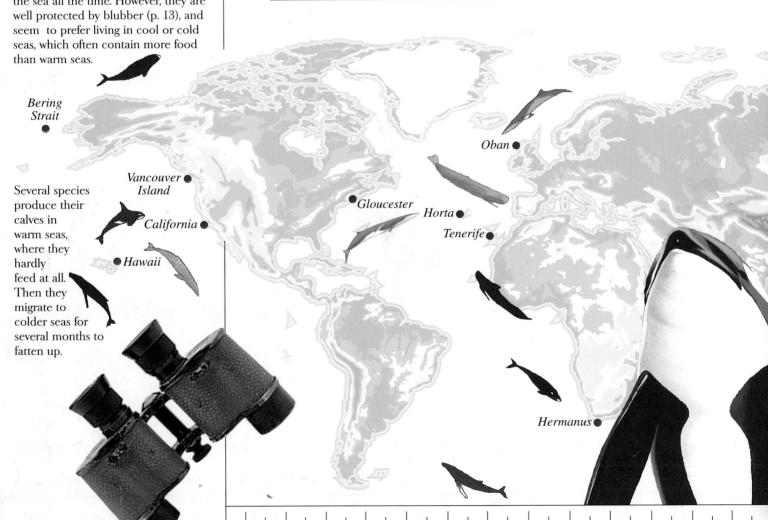

Bering Strait

Vancouver Island

California

Hawaii

Oban

Gloucester

Horta

Tenerife

Hermanus

Trailing the whales across the oceans

BERING STRAIT

Bering Strait forms a gateway between the cold North Pacific Ocean and the even colder Arctic Ocean. Bowheads, belugas and several other species of whales and dolphins pass through it twice yearly, northward in spring and southward in autumn.

HAWAII

Hawaii, a chain of deep volcanic islands, provides warm sheltered waters and good feeding for northern humpback whales.

VANCOUVER ISLAND

Vancouver Island lies off the west coast of British Columbia, Canada. The narrow passage, Johnstone Strait, between island and mainland is the year-round home of several families of orcas (killer whales).

CALIFORNIA

California has a coastline that gray whales follow twice each year. They swim southeastward in autumn from summer feeding grounds off Alaska to winter breeding grounds along the Mexican coast, returning northwestward in spring with the new season's calves.

SHIKOKU

Shikoku, one of Japan's southern islands, lies close to underwater banks that provide feeding for Bryde's whales, minke whales and Risso's and other species of dolphins.

GLOUCESTER

Gloucester, Massachusetts. A rich feeding area in Massachusetts Bay, off the New England coast, brings fin, minke and humpback and rare Atlantic right whales close inshore, together with several species of dolphins.

OBAN

Oban, Scotland. The Hebrides Islands, off Scotland's northwest coast, provide a late summer haven for minke whales, harbor porpoises and several species of dolphins.

HORTA

Horta, Azores islands. Northern sperm whales congregate among these mid-Atlantic islands throughout the year, feeding in the deep canyons between the island groups. They become especially plentiful in summer and autumn, when they can easily be spotted from the cliff-tops.

TENERIFE

Tenerife, largest of the volcanic Canary Islands, is home to several groups of pilot whales - large dolphins that swim in pods, or groups. Off the southwest corner of the island they come close inshore, where they can easily be seen from cliffs or small boats, often accompanied by bottlenose dolphins.

HERMANUS

Hermanus, South Africa. Southern right whales that feed far offshore in summer congregate in winter in warm, shallow bays along the coast of South Africa. There they court, mate and produce their calves, often only a few yards beyond the surf, and easily visible from cliff-tops and beaches.

KAIKOURA

Kaikoura, New Zealand. One or two miles offshore, over very deep water, southern sperm whales pass throughout the year on north-south migrations between warm and cold waters. Shallows closer inshore are a playground for Hector's, dusky and bottlenose dolphins.

GERLACHE STRAIT

Gerlache Strait, Antarctica. Though ice-covered for nine to ten months each year, this wide channel off the Antarctic Peninsula opens briefly in summer to provide a rich feeding ground for penguins, seals, and southern humpback, minke and bottlenose whales.

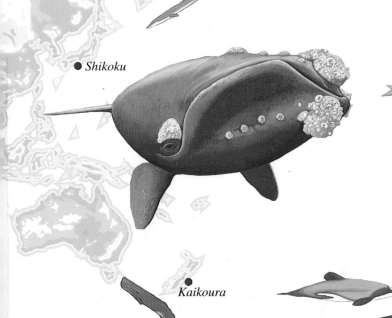

● Shikoku

Kaikoura

INTRODUCING CETACEANS

"Cetaceans" [sih-tay-shuns] is the scientific name for whales, dolphins and porpoises, from the Greek word for whale. There are about 73 different kinds of cetaceans in the world, all basically similar to each other, and sufficiently different from all other animals to form a separate group.

Though their ancestors were land animals, all cetaceans spend all their lives in water. Most live in the sea. Just a few live in rivers and lakes. In these pages we see the biggest whales, several of the middle-size ones, and some of the dolphins and porpoises. These are all species that you might be lucky enough to see when you go whale watching.

BIG AND SMALL

The biggest cetaceans – southern blue whales – grow up to 108 ft. (33 m) long and weigh over 180 tons. A newborn blue whale calf may be over 23 ft. (7 m) long and weigh over 2 tons.

The smallest cetaceans – Hector's dolphins of New Zealand waters – grow to about 5 ft. (1.5 m) long and weigh as little as 77–88 lbs. (35–40 kg). At birth they measure 24 in. (60 cm) and weigh only 20 lbs. (9 kg).

WHALES, DOLPHINS AND PORPOISES

Warm-blooded, air-breathing, intelligent, playful, streamlined for speed and efficiency in the water – these are the sea mammals we call cetaceans.

Blue whale

Sperm whale

Bottlenose whale

Hector's dolphin

Common dolphin

Narwhal

Humpback whale

BREATHING AND BLOWING

Despite living in water, cetaceans have lungs, not gills, and they breathe air. To make breathing easier, the nostrils are on top of the head. This is the part that comes up to the surface first. On reaching the surface, the whale first breathes out, producing a "spout" or "blow" of water vapor that can often be seen, particularly in cold weather.

Seeing the blow, and hearing the "huff" that goes with it, are often the first signs that whales are about. When resting they float, just breaking the surface. Some species show a snout, a dorsal fin and a length of back. This makes them easier to spot than fish or other aquatic animals.

How whales evolved

LENGTHS OF CETACEANS

Blue whale	100 ft. (30 m)
Finback whale	80 ft. (25 m)
Bowhead whale	60 ft. (18 m)
Sperm whale	50 ft. (16 m)
Bryde's whale	36 ft. (11 m)
Orca whale	30 ft. (9 m)
Minke whale	26 ft. (8 m)
Bottlenose whale	23 ft. (7 m)
Narwhal	16 ft. (5 m)
Common dolphin	8 ft. (2.5 m)
Hector's dolphin	5 ft. (1.5 m)

There are two basic kinds of cetaceans, Odontocetes [oh-don-toe-seats] and Mysticetes [mice-tih-seats]. Odontocetes (the name means "toothed whales") usually have teeth. Some species have several dozen, others only a few or none at all. They feed on fish, squid and all kinds of large prey. Mysticetes ("moustached whales") have no teeth, but a strainer of baleen (p.17) or "whalebone" in their mouths, and feed by straining very small animals from the water.

There are several other differences between the two groups, which probably evolved (arose) a long time ago from two different kinds of land mammals. Many different kinds of whales are known only as fossils, for example the Archaeocete [are-kay-oh-seat]. Today we know of 64 living species of Odontocetes, and 9 living species of Mysticetes. New species are found from time to time, and there may well be other cetaceans in the sea that we have not yet discovered.

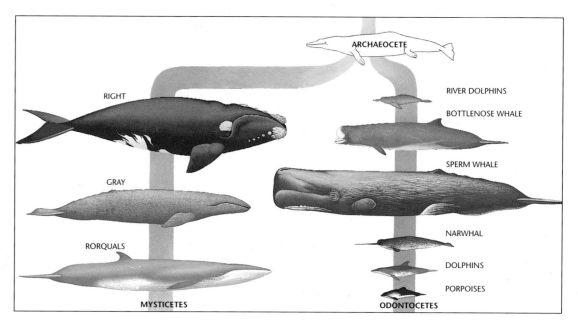

The ancestors of whales were four-legged land animals, possibly grazing animals like sheep or cattle, that took to living in water 50–70 million years ago. In time the front legs became flattened paddles, the hind legs grew smaller and disappeared, the body became long and narrow, the back muscles developed to pull the tail up and down – the way all cetaceans swim – and the tail developed flukes or fins of its own. Zygorhiza (below) is an example.

The nostrils moved upward to the top of the head, making it easier for the whale to breathe, but changing the whole shape of the face. At some stage, perhaps about 40 million years ago, the Mysticetes lost their teeth, instead growing baleen plates in the roof of the mouth, and developing enormous jaws to take in huge gulps of seawater.

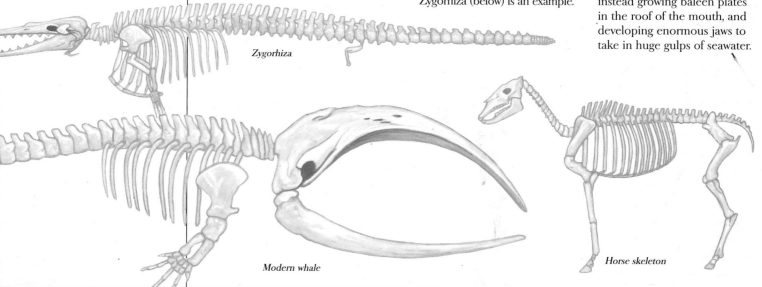

Zygorhiza

Modern whale

Horse skeleton

WHALES AT HOME

Cetaceans have developed from four-legged, land-based ancestors into sleek, streamlined creatures. Completely at home in water, they can outswim fish.

MAMMALS IN WATER

Like horses, dogs and people, cetaceans are mammals. Like all other mammals, they have warm blood, breathe air, produce their young alive, and feed them on milk. While most mammals live on land, cetaceans live in water. Some other kinds of mammals –

for example beavers, otters, seals, sea lions and walruses – feed in water but come up onto land to give birth and raise their young.

Cetaceans cannot come up on land. They have become entirely aquatic. Young cetaceans (called calves) are born into the water and swim alongside their parents immediately. A cetacean that is accidentally stranded or washed up onto a beach, like the sperm whale shown above, is almost helpless. If it cannot return to the sea, it dies (p. 38).

• *tail flukes*

SWIMMING

To swim efficiently, cetaceans have become fish-like in shape, developing a tail propeller that moves up-and-down instead of sideways, losing their hind limbs, and converting fore-limbs to flippers. These adaptations make them helpless on land, but very efficient in water.

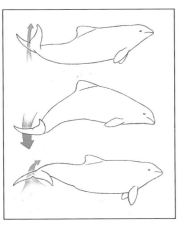

LAND MAMMALS are well adapted for living on land, but not very efficient in the water. The best Olympic swimmer cannot swim half as well as a fish. In water we quickly lose heat. Even a warmed swimming pool makes us feel chilly after an hour or so. Our skin becomes waterlogged. Under water we cannot breathe or hold our breath for long. We cannot dive deep without bottles of compressed air; we cannot see, hear or smell properly; and we are liable to choke if we try to eat under water.

These problems, shared by all land-based mammals that enter water, are the problems that whales, dolphins and porpoises have had to overcome. The pictures and notes on this page tell how they have done so.

Belugas feeding on the surface.

HOW FAST?

Whether swimming long distances or sprinting to catch fish, cetaceans seem to glide without effort through the water. Big whales on migration average 10–12 miles (16–20 km) per hour. Hunters report that individual rorquals can speed up to 18 miles (30 km) per hour for short distances, but soon tire. Dolphins seem happy to ride the bow-wave of boats

dorsal fin •

Black dolphin

traveling at up to 9 miles (15 km) per hour, and some have kept up at twice that speed, though again not for long.

flippers •

HOW DEEP?

Most whales live close to the surface, where much of their food is found, and seldom dive at all. Only a few species dive deep for their food. Sperm whales hold the record for deep diving. They have been caught up with submarine cables on the seabed more than 3280 feet (1000 m) deep, and recorded by sound location at twice that depth. Even more remarkably, they can stay down for over an hour at a time. Bottlenose whales too are deep divers. We do not know how deep they go, but they have been known to stay down for two hours or more.

WATERPROOFING

A cetacean's skin is soft and rubbery, and completely waterproof. It stretches and dimples when the animal is swimming, reducing friction and smoothing the flow of water. Cetaceans maintain a high body temperature, around 100–102°F (38–39°C).

Whales have a soft, smooth skin that is easily damaged when they are out of water.

Fur would be useless to them, as once it becomes waterlogged, it no longer insulates. Instead they have developed a layer of fat

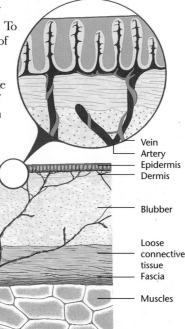

(blubber) under the skin, which keeps the heat in when they are resting, or lets it out when they are active (see Keeping warm and cool). The nostrils on top of the head make it easy for the cetacean to breathe at the surface. They can hold their breath very much longer than land mammals, and carry more dissolved oxygen in their blood and muscles, so they do not have to breathe so often.

Keeping warm and cool

To keep a high body temperature, mammals need far more food than cold-blooded animals. However, warm blood makes them very much more efficient, and able to live almost anywhere. Cetaceans are as efficient in warm water as in cold. They have no fur, but their "blubber" – the fat that they carry under their skin – is a very efficient kind of insulation that keeps them both warm and cool.

When they are in warm seas, or swimming very actively and producing a lot of heat in their muscles, they tend to overheat – just as you do if you run hard on a hot day. To cool down they flush a lot of blood through their blubber to their skin, and shed heat into the sea – like a runner taking his shirt off and letting the air cool him down. In cold water they withdraw blood from their blubber and skin. This is like putting on an overcoat.

They let their surface temperature fall, but keep a high temperature in their muscles and the rest of their body.

Whales that swim in tropical seas and dive deep for their food pass within a few minutes from warm waters to cold, then back to warm when they return to the surface. However active they are, and whether the sea around them is warm or cold, their internal body temperature remains just the same.

Vein
Artery
Epidermis
Dermis

Blubber

Loose connective tissue
Fascia

Muscles

DIVING

All cetaceans swim completely under water, and some dive deep. However, all must come to the surface from time to time to take in fresh air and breathe out used air from their lungs. While resting at the surface they breathe only once every few minutes. When swimming fast, they have to breathe more often. Some that normally feed at the surface can dive for five to ten minutes at a time. Others that hunt in deep water for their food stay down much longer, even for hours at a time.

Humpback whale about to dive.

DIVING DEEP

A man diving even to 160 ft. (50 m) must take down a cylinder of air to breathe from. Otherwise the weight of water crushes his chest. When he returns to the surface, there is a danger that, under reduced pressure, nitrogen dissolved in his blood will bubble out and cause crippling damage to his joints and brain. The diving whales dive very much deeper without these problems. They have relatively small lungs and take very little air down with them. The oxygen they need to keep moving is held in their blood, not in their lungs. So they can dive deep and stay below for as long as an hour without suffocating and return to the surface without danger of gas bubbles.

1,000 metres (3,280 ft).

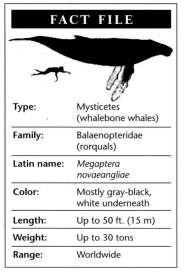

FACT FILE

Type:	Mysticetes (whalebone whales)
Family:	Balaenopteridae (rorquals)
Latin name:	*Megaptera novaeangliae*
Color:	Mostly gray-black, white underneath
Length:	Up to 50 ft. (15 m)
Weight:	Up to 30 tons
Range:	Worldwide

HUMPBACK WHALES

Huge flippers, knobbly faces and a hump under the dorsal fin make humpbacks different from all other whales. Black on top and white underneath, slow-moving, inquisitive but gentle, they are good whales to watch in all the world's oceans.

DISTRIBUTION
Though found all over the world, humpbacks tend to gather in shallow, warm tropical waters for breeding in winter, then migrate to deeper, cold waters of polar regions for summer feeding.

HUMPBACK WHALES are mainly dark gray or black, with patches of pale gray or white under the chin and throat. The flippers may be black, white or mottled both on top and below. The big tail flukes are usually black on top with a pattern of black and white underneath.

Humpbacks are the fattest, roundest and slowest-moving of the rorquals. When they are about, you see first their long, dark backs in the water, with a dorsal fin standing on a low hump.

them. The head stays low in the water, and the "blow" is shaped like a bush, rising 6–9 feet (2–3 m) from the surface. Closeup you may see the long flippers, sticking out like huge oars on either side. Up to 16 feet (5 m) long, they are one-third the length of the whale itself, and up to 3 feet (1m) across. No other species has flippers that seem quite so long or broad. Often the flippers are white. You may see them flashing under the water.

If you approach in a boat, the humpbacks will probably see you and swim close for a few minutes. They seem curious, and may come right alongside.

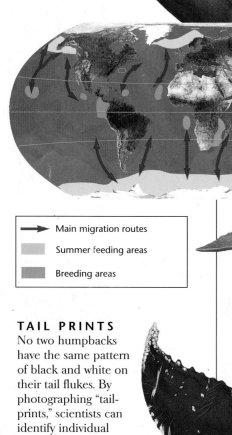

→	Main migration routes
	Summer feeding areas
	Breeding areas

TAIL PRINTS
No two humpbacks have the same pattern of black and white on their tail flukes. By photographing "tail-prints," scientists can identify individual whales and find them again in different parts of their ranges. Several thousand humpback tail flukes have now been photographed for this purpose, and many whales identified from them.

When they dive, they bend their backs like an arch and the hump becomes more prominent - hence the name. When they "sound" (dive deeply), they raise the big tail flukes out of the water.

In calm weather you may hear humpacks blowing before you see

Then you notice the bumps and knobs arranged in rows along the nose and chin. There are similar knobs along the flippers too. Sometimes you see a coarse bristle or hair growing from the middle of each knob. These are probably sensitive to touch, and may tell the whale when it is passing through shoals of small fish or plankton.

Close encounters with humpbacks

DIFFERENT KINDS

There are three main stocks, in the North Pacific Ocean, the North Atlantic Ocean and the Antarctic Ocean. Though similar and closely related, humpbacks of different stocks seem to keep separate from each other and seldom meet.

An exuberant humpback breaching in the North Atlantic Ocean - a good reason to keep your distance.

FEEDING

Humpbacks feed on plankton (mostly small, shrimp-like crustaceans) and small fish, which they filter from the sea-water. The whale swims into a shoal of food with its mouth open. The pleated throat drops to expand the mouth cavity, and the lower jaw closes, trapping a huge amount of water with the food contained in it. Then the whale presses the water out through its baleen filter (p. 17), leaving the food behind. Some humpbacks first swim in spirals through and around the shoals, causing the plankton or fish to pack closer together and make richer mouthfuls.

The best places to see humpbacks are in their breeding and feeding areas and along known migration routes between. They spend their winters mainly in warm, shallow waters, for example off Hawaii in the North Pacific Ocean, the West Indies and Bermuda in the western Atlantic Ocean, the Cape Verde Islands in the eastern Atlantic, and Tonga, Fiji, Samoa and Ecuador in the southern Pacific. There they breed, some producing calves, others courting and mating. There are good centers for whale-spotting in many of these areas.

At the end of winter - March to May in the Northern Hemisphere, September to November in the south - they move toward colder waters. North Pacific humpbacks swim north toward the Bering Strait, North Atlantic humpbacks toward Labrador, Greenland, Iceland and Svalbard. Southern Hemisphere humpbacks swim south toward Antarctica. Some can be seen close inshore along their migration routes, for example off New England, Baja California, Norway and Japan in the Northern Hemisphere, and South Africa, South America, New Zealand and Australia in the south.

South Pacific Ocean

SANTIAGO •

SOUTH AMERICA

South Atlantic Ocean

The Falkland Islands

Antarctic Peninsula

ANTARCTICA

Tourists on Arctic and Antarctic cruise ships often see humpbacks on their feeding grounds. Sometimes they are solitary, but more often in family groups - mothers with single half-grown calves. At several points along these coasts, whaling stations used to operate, hunting the whales as they migrated past. Now whale hunters have mostly been replaced by whale watchers, who take you out in launches to see the whales go past.

(Above left) Whales often make use of channels cut by icebrakers. (Above) Humpback emerging to watch whale watchers.

KEEP YOUR DISTANCE

Humpback whales are usually gentle and often seem interested when a boat comes near. They may even scratch their noses on the hull. However, they are VERY BIG. A flick of the tail from even a friendly humpback could cause a nasty accident. Make sure you stop at least two whale's-lengths away. Do not chase them. Watch them quietly, and let them go on their own way.

BOWHEAD & RIGHT WHALES

Whalers always felt they were in luck when they found one of these fat, slow-moving whales. Easy to catch, carrying thick blubber and long, valuable whalebone, they were the "right" whales to catch.

FACT FILE

GREENLAND RIGHT AND BOWHEAD WHALE

Type:	Mysticetes (whalebone whales)
Family:	Balaenidae (right whales)
Latin name:	*Balaena mysticetus*
Color:	Black or dark slate gray, usually with a white or yellowish patch on the lower jaw, barnacled chin.
Length:	Up to 60 ft. (18 m)
Weight:	Up to 100 tons
Range:	Arctic Ocean and cold waters of the northern Pacific and Atlantic oceans

BLACK RIGHT WHALE

Type:	Mysticetes (whalebone whales)
Family:	Balaenidae (right whales)
Latin name:	*Balaena glacialis*
Color:	Black or dark gray-brown, with gray or white patches between the flippers, barnacled face
Length:	46–50 ft. (14–15.5 m)
Weight:	50–100 tons
Range:	Temperate and cool waters of the North Pacific and Atlantic oceans, and of the South Pacific, Atlantic and Indian oceans

IS IT A RIGHT WHALE?

Right whales swim in temperate and cold waters, often close inshore. Big, tubby, slow-moving whales, they are much fatter than their sleek, streamlined rorqual cousins. They bumble and roll through the water like barrels, feeding at the surface, seldom deep-diving, and sending up double spouts or blows. They have large flippers and tail flukes, no dorsal fin and a huge mouth containing whalebone plates over 6.5 ft. (2 m) long. Their faces nearly always carry patches of gray barnacles.

RIGHT WHALES are some of the easiest whales to watch. Living in temperate and cool waters of both hemispheres, they swim slowly, come right inshore and do not seem to worry about being watched. Sadly, these qualities made them very easy to hunt, and for several hundred years whalers have harpooned them - even caught them in nets - close inshore from rowing and sailing boats.

harpoon guns. Not surprisingly, by the end of the 19th century, right whales of all kinds were almost exterminated.

Today, the few thousand that remain are protected all over the world, except in parts of the Arctic, where local people are allowed to take a few each year. Bowheads are becoming more common in the North Pacific Ocean. Greenland and black right whales are still fairly rare in the North Atlantic Ocean, but may be increasing.

Southern right whale with calf

Early hunters prized them particularly because they contain more fat than most other whales, and do not sink when they die. Their baleen was much longer than in other whales. Formerly used for making all sorts of things that we now make in plastics or spring steel (for example brush bristles and umbrella ribs), it was at times even more valuable than their oil. Catching them was easier still from steamboats with explosive

Southern stocks have certainly increased since whaling stopped. Like many other whales, right whales swim to colder waters in summer, to feed hungrily on the swarms of crustaceans, then spend winters in warmer waters, where they give birth to their calves.

Looking for right whales

DIFFERENT KINDS

Greenland right and bowhead whales, the Arctic species, are very similar to each other. "Bowhead" is a local name given to those that swim off Alaska and the northern Pacific Ocean. The different types of black right whales, the species of temperate and cool waters, are also very similar to each other. This is surprising, because those that live in the North Pacific can seldom meet or mix with those from the North Atlantic, and - so far as we know - neither is likely to meet black right whales that live in the southern oceans.

Bowhead whale

A PYGMY WHALE

The pigmy right whale, *Caperea marginata,* is a different kind of right whale that lives in southern temperate waters and sometimes appears off South Africa, New Zealand, Australia and the Falkland Islands. Pale blue-gray, less than half the length of black right whales, these move in small groups of up to seven or eight, feeding like true right whales on crustaceans. We know very little about them, but they sometimes come close inshore, especially around Australia. Keep an eye open for pale small whales with the typical bowed lower jaw of a right whale - you may just be lucky.

Pygmy right whale

BALEEN

Like all other mysticete or whalebone whales, right whales feed in swarms of small prey - mostly shrimp-like crustaceans of the zooplankton. The mouths are enormous, opening wide enough to hold a small car. From the roof of the mouth hang as many as 300 long triangular plates of horny baleen, matted at the inner edges. These make a strainer like a huge, very rough doormat, which allows the seawater to pass through but holds back the thousands of crustaceans - which can then be swallowed.

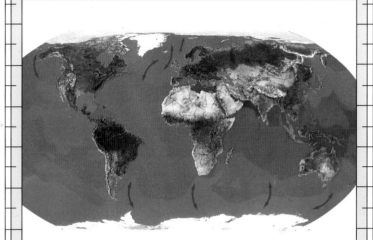

Southern right whales spend summers feeding in the open ocean, and in winters seek the calm of warm sheltered bays to court, mate and produce their calves. Southern Africa has many such bays, where the whales come close inshore between June and November, staying for several days or weeks at a time. Often you see them lazing, or occasionally rolling and tumbling, just beyond the surf. People with houses along the cliffs watch them through their kitchen windows and recognize particular whales that return to the same place each year. Mating and calving take place in several other bays along the coast.

Southern right whales also can be seen off the coast of South America, for example at Peninsula Valdés, Argentine Patagonia, and at several points along the western and southern Australian coasts. They have been known to visit some of New Zealand's southern islands, for example Campbell Island, where visiting cruise ships sometimes encounter them. Northern black right whales are becoming more common along the coasts of New England, for example off Gloucester, Mass., and the Gulf of Maine, providing an occasional bonus for passengers on whale-watching cruises.

Greenland right whales and Alaskan bowheads are seen every year by coast-living Inuit, and by biologists who count them from coastal lookout points during their spring and autumn migrations. The Inuit are allowed to take a small number for food.

During their annual migrations many of these whales swim close inshore, and they like to produce their calves in sheltered bays, where the water is warm and still. These are the best places to find them.

Southern right whale with calf, feeding at the surface.

FACT FILE

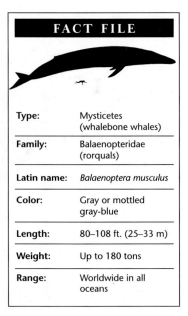

Type:	Mysticetes (whalebone whales)
Family:	Balaenopteridae (rorquals)
Latin name:	*Balaenoptera musculus*
Color:	Gray or mottled gray-blue
Length:	80–108 ft. (25–33 m)
Weight:	Up to 180 tons
Range:	Worldwide in all oceans

HOW MANY ARE THERE?

It is impossible to count blue whales. Scientists can only estimate their numbers past and present. A hundred years ago, before the serious hunting began, there were probably about 230,000. In 1967, when the hunting ended, only about 6,000 were left. Now we hope they are increasing again. A recent estimate is about 14,000.

FEEDING

Like all other rorquals, blue whales feed on zooplankton - mainly tiny shrimp-like crustaceans that swarm in cold waters. When a whale finds a shoal of plankton, it opens its mouth (wide enough to hold a motor coach) and enlarges it further by expanding the pleats of the throat. This brings in several hundred gallons of seawater, containing thousands of shrimps. Closing its jaws, the whale presses the water through the mat of baleen and out through the sides of its mouth, leaving the shrimps behind. Then an enormous tongue rounds up the shrimps and pushes them down the throat.

BLUE WHALES

Biggest of all the whales, heavier than 15 great elephants, these are the largest and heaviest animals alive today. They may even be the biggest that have ever lived. Sadly, many thousands have been hunted and killed for their oil.

LIKE MANY OTHER LARGE WHALES, blue whales divide their time between cold seas and warm. Cold seas provide better feeding, but warm seas are kinder for calves during their first few months of life. So females keep up their strength during pregnancy by feeding at the colder end of their range, but give birth to their calves in the warmth.

In the Southern Hemisphere, most calves are born about May. Though 23 feet (7 m) long at birth, the newborn calves have little fat on them, and would quickly die if surrounded by icy sea.

Females on average grow slightly larger than males. By their fifth or sixth year the young whales are almost full-sized, and ready to mate and have calves of their own. They mate at the warmer ends of their range. That is where we sometimes see small groups of blue whales leaping and splashing in the water, the males courting and fighting over the females. Blue whales live 30–40 years, each female producing 10 to 12 calves in her lifetime.

Big whales have big appetites. A large blue whale needs 4–5 tons of food each summer day to build up its fat reserves.

Feeding on their mother's rich milk, they grow very quickly. Within two or three months they have doubled in length, and in five or six months they are big enough to follow their mothers on their first long migration. By the time they reach the cold waters they are ready to feed themselves.

Their main food is the tiny shrimp-like crustaceans of the zooplankton. Some patches of warm seas are rich enough to support large swarms of zooplankton, but the supply is never certain. So most blue whales migrate in spring to the colder parts of the ocean, where they can be sure of three or four months' good feeding.

Finding blue whales

Blue whales are found in all the world's oceans. There are, and have always been, far more south of the Equator than in the north, and the two stocks never seem to mix. Northern blue whales winter in warm tropical waters of the Pacific and Atlantic oceans. In summer those of the Pacific Ocean swim northward as far as Japan, Alaska and the Bering Strait. Those of the Atlantic reach Iceland and the Norwegian Sea. Southern stocks make similar north-south migrations between the tropics and the Antarctic Ocean, many reaching as far south as the Antarctic pack ice.

Despite their wide distribution, meeting a blue whale is very much a matter of luck. There are not many of them. They tend to be loners or to swim in small groups of two or three, and they travel in mid-ocean rather than along the coasts.

We know very few areas, at either end of their long migrations, where they always gather. However, whale-watching groups have spotted them in localities as far apart as the Azores, New England, the Gulf of St. Lawrence, Iceland, northern Norway, Sri Lanka, Alaska and California, and cruise ships in the far south occasionally see them on the fringes of Antarctica.

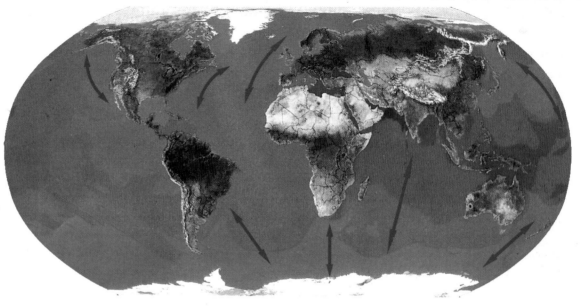

A blue whale spouting. The spout may be over 13ft (4 m) tall.

DIFFERENT KINDS

Though blue whales look very much the same all the world over, the biggest have generally been found in the southern oceans. Those that live in the North Atlantic and North Pacific oceans and those that live south of the Equator quite probably never meet. Even the blue whales of the southern Indian, Atlantic and Pacific oceans seem to belong to separate populations that seldom if ever come into contact.

IS IT A BLUE WHALE?

There is no mistaking blue whales. Found all over the world, they are seldom blue (more likely to be dull gray on top, sometimes with a yellowish sheen, and pale greenish gray underneath), but they are enormous – the biggest animals you will ever see, as long as three motor-coaches, and twice as fat. There is a small dorsal fin, set two-thirds of the way along the body. The flippers are broad and pointed, the tail flukes up to 20 feet (6 m) across. The undersides of the mouth and throat are pleated with huge, longitudinal grooves.

FACT FILE

FINBACK WHALES

Type:	Mysticetes (whalebone whales)
Family:	Balaenopteridae (rorquals)
Latin name:	*Balaenoptera physalus*
Color:	Dark gray or brown, often with pale stripes or "V"-shaped markings behind the flippers; pale underside, right lower jaw and baleen often white
Length:	60–80 ft. (18–25 m)
Weight:	Up to 80 tons
Range:	Temperate and cold waters of both hemispheres: more in south than north

SEI WHALES

Type:	Mysticetes (whalebone whales)
Family:	Balaenopteridae (rorquals)
Latin name:	*Balaenoptera borealis*
Color:	Dark gray above, pale below
Length:	40–56 ft. (12–17 m)
Weight:	Up to 30 tons
Range:	Tropical to polar waters of both hemispheres; more in north than south

BRYDE'S WHALES

Type:	Mysticetes (whalebone whales)
Family:	Balaenopteridae (rorquals)
Latin name:	*Balaenoptera edeni*
Color:	Dark gray with pale bands above, pale to white below
Length:	40–46 ft. (12–14 m)
Weight:	Up to 26 tons
Range:	Tropical and subtropical waters of both hemispheres

MINKE WHALES

Type:	Mysticetes (whalebone whales)
Family:	Balaenopteridae (rorquals)
Latin name:	*Balaenoptera acutorostrata*
Colour:	Dark gray to black above, paler below; most northern and a few southern individuals have a white bar on either flipper
Length:	23–33 ft. (7–10 m)
Weight:	About 10 tons
Range:	Tropical, temperate and polar waters of both hemispheres

THE SMALLER RORQUALS

Fin, sei, Bryde's and minke whales, though smaller cousins of the blue whale, are still among the biggest animals you will ever see.

RORQUALS, the largest, slimmest, fastest-moving whales, come in a range of sizes. Blue whales (p. 18) are usually the largest and heaviest. Finback or fin whales, the next biggest, come closest to blue whales in length, but are always slimmer. On average they weigh only two-thirds as much. Sei and Bryde's whales are very much smaller - about half the length of blues, much thinner and on average about half the weight. Minke whales, the babies of the family, are relatively tiny, one-third the length of blues and less than a fifteenth of the weight.

These are all baleen whales, which feed by filtering small fish and plankton from the sea. All have a dorsal fin, and deep pleats or grooves from lower jaw to stomach, allowing their throat to expand like a balloon when they feed. The main differences between them are in body size and small details of head shape and body coloring. When you see them at sea, there are usually just one or two together, seldom more than four or five in a group, though where food is plentiful there may be several small groups feeding in the same area.

FIN WHALE
Second-largest of all the whales, finback or fin are very similar to blues, and only slightly smaller. They get their name from the relatively large, hooked dorsal fin, set far back along the body.

MINKE WHALE
The smallest rorquals, these are gray or black above and paler below, but are almost white underneath, others gray. Some have pale swirling bands above the flippers, other none at all.

Where do we find them?

THE SMALLER RORQUALS

These are four kinds of fast-moving baleen whales, all closely related to blue whales. They feed by straining plankton and small fish from surface waters. Though smaller than blue whales, they are still very big animals. Finback, or fin whales, are almost as big as blues. Sei (pronounced "say") and Bryde's (pronounced "brooders") whales are only half as long. Minkes, (pronounced "minky") the smallest and slimmest of the family, weigh as much as two or three elephants.

SEI WHALE

These are similar in shape and color to blue and fin whales, with a similar ridge on the head. However, they are only half their length and much thinner.

FIN WHALES

Look out for a very large whale (remember, almost as big as a blue), with white or pale gray undersides of flippers and tail flukes, and a pale patch on the right side of the lower jaw. The top of the head has a prominent ridge. They are found in warm-temperate and cool waters of both hemispheres in winter. Some stay year-round in warm waters, but most make their way polewards in spring, to feed and fatten in the Arctic and Antarctic. So your best chance of seeing them is in cold waters in summertime, for example off Iceland, Greenland, Alaska or eastern Canada. About 20,000 live in the Northern Hemisphere, and possibly five times as many in the south, so Antarctic waters are a good bet too.

SEI WHALES

Their name is based on the Norwegian name *seje,* for coalfish, because each year the whales and fish appear at the same time off the Norwegian coast. In winter they live in warm temperate regions. Their calves, over 13 feet (4 m) long at birth, are born in warm seas, and migrate with their mothers to cold waters in spring and early summer. Short baleen plates make a finer network or mesh, suggesting that these whales feed on the very smallest crustaceans. A medium-sized rorqual in cold waters is almost bound to be a sei whale. Look out for them along the Arctic and Antarctic fringes, off Norway, Canada (Hudson Strait and Nova Scotia are popular feeding grounds), southern Greenland or Antarctica. They are not uncommon - about 17,000 of them live in the Northern Hemisphere, and possibly twice as many in the south.

BRYDE'S WHALES

The first specimens of this whale to be studied in detail were caught off South Africa, and named for a Norwegian whaler who set up the first whaling station there. They are mainly tropical and temperate whales. You seldom find them in cold water, and never among ice. Their baleen is much coarser than that of other rorquals. They probably eat more fish than plankton. There are not many of them - possibly about 20,000 altogether - so you seldom see them except on well-known feeding grounds. Whale watchers look for them off southern Japan (where former whale hunters now take people out in boats to see them), and off Southern California and South Africa.

Bryde's whales have three ridges on the head.

MINKE WHALES

These are by far the commonest rorquals. There are probably over 120,000 in the Northern Hemisphere and almost 400,000 in the south, so your chances of seeing one are good. Any small rorqual around 9 m (30 ft) long that is clearly not a calf alongside its mother can only be a minke whale. The front of the head is flat and sharply pointed like a pike or spear. Another common name for this species is "piked" whale. You see them mainly in temperate and cool waters in winter and in polar waters, even ice-bound, in summer. Eastern Canada, New England, Iceland, northwest Scotland, Norway and Japan are likely places, and several are seen on almost every Antarctic cruise.

Sei whale

Fin whale

Minke whale

Bryde's whale

BRYDE'S WHALE

Though very similar to sei whales, they have three sharp ridges on their head, and are usually found closer to land.

GRAY WHALES

Gray whales migrate each year along both shores of the North Pacific Ocean, as far south as Baja California in the east, and Korea in the west. Along the California coast, whale watchers look out for them from November to March.

FACT FILE

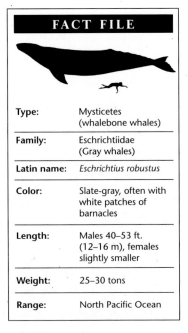

Type:	Mysticetes (whalebone whales)
Family:	Eschrichtiidae (Gray whales)
Latin name:	*Eschrichtius robustus*
Color:	Slate-gray, often with white patches of barnacles
Length:	Males 40–53 ft. (12–16 m), females slightly smaller
Weight:	25–30 tons
Range:	North Pacific Ocean

HOW TO IDENTIFY THEM

These are long, slender whales, silvery-to-dull gray, with surface mottled by scars and patches of barnacles. The throat has only two to four short grooves (compare this with the many long grooves of rorquals, for example blue whales, p.18). The baleen is short and usually white or yellowish. The flippers are short, broad and pointed, and the dorsal fin is little more than a small bump.

THOUGH CLOSELY RELATED to rorquals, gray whales form a family of their own, with just the one species. These are big whales, looking very much like rorquals but usually more slender and streamlined, with a smaller mouth, and upper jaws lined with short plates of baleen, matted together like a stiff brush.

They lack the long throat grooves that we always see in humpbacks and rorquals, which indicate a different way of feeding.

Gray whales have double nostrils, and blow out two separate jets of spray, up to 15 feet (4.5 m) high, that from the front appear heart-shaped. In a dive, the small dorsal fin, or hump, appears, followed by a row of tiny humps along the top of the tail. The tail flukes are triangular with rounded trailing edges and a sharp V-notch.

LIVELY WHALES

Among the most active of all large whales, gray whales migrate almost 12,000 miles (20,000 km) each year from Arctic to tropical waters and back. They move alone or in small groups of up to five or six. Two or three females may travel northward together with their calves, perhaps for protection against killer whales. While traveling they often breach (jump clear of the water), and they seem always ready to come and investigate small boats, sticking their noses far out of the water to scan the surface.

Where rorquals fill their huge mouths and throats with plankton-filled seawater (p.18), and blow the water out to leave the plankton behind, gray whales feed by scooping up mud from the seabed, and filtering small shrimp-like creatures from it.

Living mostly in shallow water, they seldom dive very deep. Very curious animals, gray whales allow boats to come quite close - close enough for us to see that their mottled gray skin is covered with barnacles and whale lice. These are two different kinds of crustaceans (animals related to shrimps, see below right) that travel with the whales and live on their surface, apparently without harming them.

Gray whales used to live in both the Atlantic and the Pacific oceans. Hunters found them easy to catch and kill, so today only the Pacific stocks remain. A few are still taken each year off Siberia, but since 1946 the main stocks on both sides of the ocean have been protected. Off the United States coast gray whales are once again plentiful, and thousands of people watch them every year in their annual migrations north and south.

Left: A grey whale about to make a deep dive.

The long migration

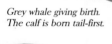

Gray whales like to see what is going on at the surface.

CALVING

Calves are born in the warm waters at the southern end of the whales' migrations. Newly born gray whales are 15 feet (4.5 m) long at birth, with dark gray skin that becomes lighter as they grow. They stay close to their mothers, feeding on rich milk. Within two months of being born, they are ready to start their first long journey north.

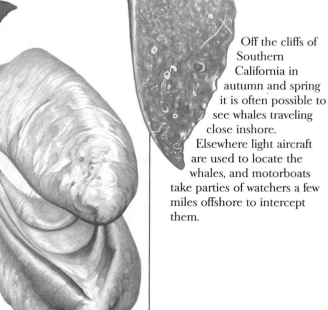

Grey whale giving birth. The calf is born tail-first.

Gray whales spend summer in the rich, cold waters of the Arctic Ocean close to the Bering Strait. In late September and early October they start to move south. A small population, possibly no more than a few hundred, trek southwestward past Kamchatka and the northern islands of Japan, as far south as Korea by late November. A much bigger population, perhaps 15–20,000, head southeastward through the Gulf of Alaska to the coasts of Oregon and California, reaching Baja California (Mexico) by late December.

At the southern ends of their migration the females give birth to their calves. Here too the whales court and mate. Females feed their calves on milk, but adults take little or no food during their stay in southern waters. From early February they start to move north again, reaching the Arctic by May or June.

During the winter months of December to March, whale watchers visit mothers and young calves in the sheltered bays of Baja California, swimming and canoeing among them.

Off the cliffs of Southern California in autumn and spring it is often possible to see whales traveling close inshore. Elsewhere light aircraft are used to locate the whales, and motorboats take parties of watchers a few miles offshore to intercept them.

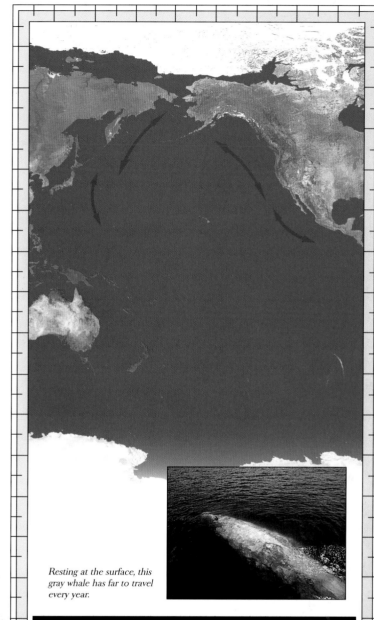

Resting at the surface, this gray whale has far to travel every year.

BARNACLES AND LICE

Barnacles are crustaceans (related to crabs and shrimps) that settle on rocks, ships and other underwater surfaces, form protective shells around themselves and live by filtering food particles from the water. Some settle on whales, digging themselves into the skin and filtering the water as it flows past. Whale lice are small crab-like creatures that scuttle among the barnacles, hanging on with sharp claws and feeding on skin and other scraps of food. Whales often rub themselves against rocks, possibly because the barnacles and lice make them feel itchy. However, neither of these passengers seems to harm them.

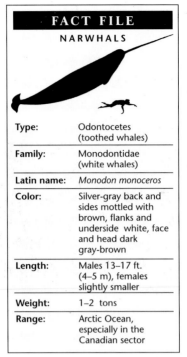

FACT FILE	
NARWHALS	

Type:	Odontocetes (toothed whales)
Family:	Monodontidae (white whales)
Latin name:	*Monodon monoceros*
Color:	Silver-gray back and sides mottled with brown, flanks and underside white, face and head dark gray-brown
Length:	Males 13–17 ft. (4–5 m), females slightly smaller
Weight:	1–2 tons
Range:	Arctic Ocean, especially in the Canadian sector

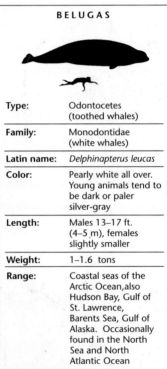

BELUGAS	
Type:	Odontocetes (toothed whales)
Family:	Monodontidae (white whales)
Latin name:	*Delphinapterus leucas*
Color:	Pearly white all over. Young animals tend to be dark or paler silver-gray
Length:	Males 13–17 ft. (4–5 m), females slightly smaller
Weight:	1–1.6 tons
Range:	Coastal seas of the Arctic Ocean, also Hudson Bay, Gulf of St. Lawrence, Barents Sea, Gulf of Alaska. Occasionally found in the North Sea and North Atlantic Ocean

UNICORNS

When ivory traders first brought narwhal tusks to Europe from the Arctic, people thought they were horns of unicorns, and paid a lot of money for them. They could be carved in figures and ornaments and set with jewels. Later, when they became more common, small ones were bound with silver or gold and made into maces and walking sticks. Larger ones became lamp stands and bedposts. Look out for them in antique shops and estates.

NARWHALS AND BELUGAS

These are small, sociable whales that live in the coldest northern seas. You see them most often among the ice floes of the Arctic, from the Arctic Ocean itself to northern Atlantic and Pacific waters.

Narwhals are the only whales that carry a tusk - a long, twisted spiral of ivory that grows from the upper jaw. Only males carry large tusks. A few have two, and some females carry smaller ones. They use them for stirring the seabed, where they hunt for fish and crustaceans. They may also use them in threat display or mock fighting. Narwhals have occasionally been reported to use their tusks in attacking and ramming small boats, but this is unlikely. Having been hunted for thousands of years, narwhals are generally shy, keeping to themselves and staying away from people.

They travel in small bands of six to a dozen, often a single large male with several females and calves. Sometimes, especially in late summer, several bands get together to form larger gatherings for courtship and mating. They make a lot of noise, including clicks and grunts that you can hear quite clearly at the surface. Bands tend to move close to the shore, feeding in shallow water and avoiding heavy pack ice.

Calves are born in early spring and feed on their mother's milk for well over a year.

Belugas (the name is Russian for "white") similarly move in groups of up to a dozen, forming larger gatherings for autumn mating and producing their calves in spring. They too live mainly along the coasts, often swimming far up some of the larger rivers. Belugas sing to each other (mariners used to call them "sea canaries") and make several other sounds including clicks and clangings.

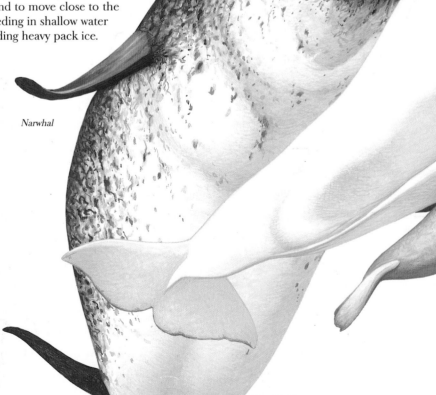

Narwhal

Ghost whales of the ice fields

Narwhals and belugas are pale, ghost-like whales of the far north. To see them together you have to travel to the Arctic Ocean, Baffin Bay, the Greenland Sea and other stretches of icy water. Narwhals are rarely found anywhere else, though occasionally they wander as far south as the North Sea. Belugas travel more widely and have been found off Japan, Massachusetts and Britain. A few years ago one swam along the Rhine to central Germany.

In the far north, both narwhals and belugas are hunted by native peoples, who know their feeding grounds, their behavior and their annual migrations better than anyone else. Scientists work with the local people to estimate numbers of both species, checking them during the spring migration from aircraft and observation posts along the shore. There are chances to see these and other Arctic species off Greenland, Alaska and Labrador, and from cruise ships in the Arctic Ocean.

Belugas close inshore.

Both belugas and narwhals are limited to the north by ice in both the Pacific and Atlantic. Belugas come further south than narwhals.

Baby belugas are gray-brown. They lose their color gradually during their first few years.

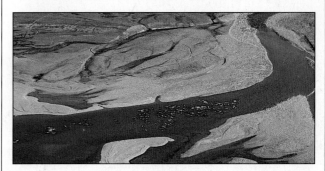

Narwhals coming up to breathe in Arctic ice.

FEEDING

Narwhals feed on salmon and herring from surface waters and flatfish, cod and crustaceans, which they stir up from the seabed. With no teeth other than their tusks, they may suck food in and swallow it whole. Belugas, which have just a few spiky teeth in both jaws, also feed on surface-living fish and on squid, fish, crustaceans and worms from the seabed.

HOW TO IDENTIFY THEM

These are whales of cold Arctic waters. Narwhals are seldom seen anywhere else, but belugas stray. Narwhals are chubby and streamlined, with round face, short flippers and small tail flukes. Males carry a distinctive tusk - actually a huge tooth up to 6 ft. (2 m) long. A few females have a smaller one. Belugas are similar in size, but pure white. They have a beaked face and a distinct neck, with relatively large flippers and tail flukes.

Group of belugas in the Canadian Arctic.

FACT FILE

KILLER WHALES
(ORCAS)

Type:	Odontocetes (toothed whales)
Family:	Delphinidae (dolphins and porpoises)
Subfamily:	Orcinae (pilot and killer whales)
Latin name:	*Orcinus orca*
Color:	Black back and sides, white underparts; white patches over eyes
Length:	Up to 35 ft. (10 m)
Weight:	Up to 9 tons
Range:	Worldwide

KILLER WHALES

Killer whales hunt the seas in packs, sometimes taking the largest whales as prey. They are actually large dolphins, living mostly on fish and squid. To visitors they are usually gentle, seldom attacking boats or man.

EVERYONE CALLS THEM WHALES, but killer whales are no more than very big dolphins, with a short, rounded head and compact, chunky body. They are conspicuously black-and-white, often showing their colors by standing upright in the water or breaching.

one large male, two or three females and one or two young. Larger groups may involve three or four large males, the rest smaller males and females with calves swimming close by. In calm weather you may hear them grunting and calling to each other with clicks and whistles. Several may

IS IT A KILLER WHALE?

Killer whales or orcas usually travel in groups, with at least one large male. The first thing you see is a disturbance - a flurry of water and several short spouts or blows. Then you see the male's black dorsal fin, standing up to 6.5 ft. (2 m) tall. There may be two or three of them, cutting through the water like sails. Then you see the smaller females, and possibly calves, all flashing unmistakably black-and-white as they twist and turn in the water.

The back and sides are black, with rounded black flippers and upper surface of tail. Many have a gray patch like a saddle behind the dorsal fin. Underneath they are white from chin to tail, with a very conspicuous white patch behind each eye, and a white patch extending halfway up the body on either flank. In polar regions they sometimes carry a film of yellow-green diatoms that turns the black to gray-blue and the white to pale yellow.

When you come close to a pack of killer whales, you see that the largest have tall dorsal fins, triangular and up to the height of a man. These are the mature males. Females and young males are smaller, with shorter fins that curve slightly backward at the point.

Normally killer whales cruise slowly in small "family" groups of up to a dozen. Small groups usually include

dive together, disappearing for less than a minute. Occasionally they dive deeper, staying under for two or three minutes at a time.

Sometimes you see much larger groups of 30-40 or more, spaced widely but all swimming slowly in the same direction.

These may be made up of several smaller groups that have come together temporarily where the fishing is good.

Large male killer whales have a dorsal fin up to 6.5 ft. (2 m) tall.

Close encounters with killers

White throat and white patches behind the eye – unmistakably a killer whale.

Female killer whale

The best places to see killer whales are in deep inshore waters, enclosed bays or between islands, where particular groups have been seen, visited or studied regularly. These will be accustomed to being watched, and less likely to swim away.

Groups of killer whales often come close inshore and can readily be approached by small boats. They quickly become used to visitors, getting on with the more important business of feeding.

In Johnstone Strait, the channel between Vancouver Island and the British Columbia mainland, several hundred killer whales have been studied as family groups for over 20 years. The scientists and boat operators know many of them as individuals and can tell you their family histories. There are good opportunities for seeing killers off Alaska, Washington, California, New England, the Azores and the Norwegian coast. Wherever other whales gather, there are usually killer whales too. They are especially plentiful in Antarctic waters. Few cruise-ship tourists return home without having seen at least one spectacular group of killer whales.

Despite their reputation for fierceness and known appetites, killer whales have seldom been reported to attack boats or humans. Nevertheless, use care when you approach them, and give them plenty of space.

Mother and calf diving

FEEDING

Killers seem usually to feed on fish and squid. However, they have 10–12 large peg-like teeth on either side of both jaws, which can be used for seizing and tearing much larger prey. They take seabirds, seals, sea lions and smaller dolphins. One killed in the North Pacific Ocean was found to have eaten 32 fully-grown seals. Another contained 13 porpoises and 15 seals.

Off Patagonia they hunt for sea lions in the surf close to the breeding grounds. In Antarctica they tip ice floes and leap onto the ice edge to grab seals and penguins. They attack and tear to pieces some of the largest whales, including gray, blue and humpback whales. Whalers who had harpooned and killed a large whale sometimes found their prey being eaten by a group of killer whales, which tore off strips of blubber and attacked the mouth and tongue.

IN CAPTIVITY

Killer whales have been caught as calves and kept in oceanaria. Like other dolphins they quickly adapt to captivity, recognizing and responding to their trainers, learning tricks and performing willingly - including having their teeth brushed by yard brooms.

A killer whale in captivity in Vancouver became very excited when nuns visited the pool, lashing the water with her tail and splashing all the onlookers. She was thought to be responding to their black and white dress. Generally, killers quickly grow too big for oceanaria and need too much food to be kept for long in captivity.

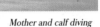

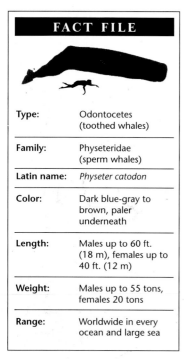

FACT FILE

Type:	Odontocetes (toothed whales)
Family:	Physeteridae (sperm whales)
Latin name:	*Physeter catodon*
Color:	Dark blue-gray to brown, paler underneath
Length:	Males up to 60 ft. (18 m), females up to 40 ft. (12 m)
Weight:	Males up to 55 tons, females 20 tons
Range:	Worldwide in every ocean and large sea

IS IT A SPERM WHALE?

These are huge, slab-sided animals, gray or brown, with rough, wrinkled skin - like old tree trunks in the sea. The head, square cut with a single nostril on the left front corner, seems to extend halfway along the body. The dorsal fin is a hump, followed by a series of bumps along the middle of the back. The flippers are broad, the tail flukes enormous. In surfacing, sperm whales stick their head out of the water first, so they look like a sinking ship. They give a massive, noisy blow, shooting out a single jet up to 17 ft. (5 m) high, followed by a succession of smaller blows. In diving, the head disappears, the hump and small bumps follow each other into the water, the tail flukes rise in the air, and the whale disappears - often to great depths.

DISTRIBUTION

Sperm whales occur in all the oceans, especially where the water is deep. They seldom come close inshore except where there is deep water, or when they are dying. Females produce their calves in tropical or temperate waters. Males visit warm waters in winter for mating, and many spend their summers in colder seas, even among the pack ice.

SPERM WHALES

Rugged gray giants with rough, wrinkled skin, these are the biggest toothed whales. They dive deep, feeding near the seabed, hunting and devouring giant squid, some longer than themselves.

SPERM WHALES of the North Atlantic Ocean feed in cool northern waters in summer - some large males as far north as the ice edge - and move south to warmer waters in winter. The mid-oceanic Azores provide good feeding grounds for them all the year round. In summer, food is plentiful for all, so bulls, females and calves are present around the islands. The winter population is mostly mature bulls. Females and calves live in warmer waters to the south.

because there is a sudden gathering of fish or squid in the area.

Calves take about 15 months to grow inside the mother. At birth they are 13 feet (4 m) long and weigh over a ton. The mothers feed them for at least a year. They start to breed aged five or six, and produce a calf about every fourth year.

Sperm whale

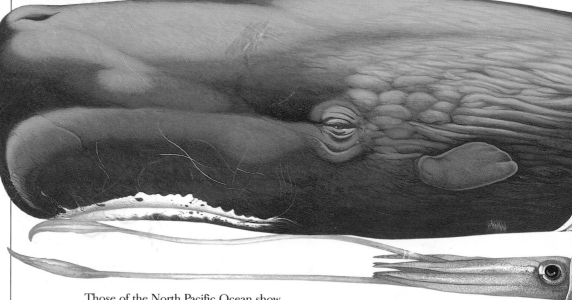

Those of the North Pacific Ocean show similar patterns of movement between Arctic and tropics. In the southern oceans there are again year-round populations in many deep-sea areas, while many bulls head southward to spend summers in cold Antarctic waters.

In warm waters they live in groups, usually of nine or ten, sometimes numbering two or three dozen. Some groups are made up entirely of young males, others mainly of females, some with calves, together with a few young males and one or two big males. The big males follow these mixed groups, trying to fight each other off and mate with the females. Occasionally much bigger groups of several hundred sperm whales are reported. We do not know why they gather like this - possibly

Giant squid - some are as long as the whales themselves.

Sperm whales have been hunted for about 300 years, mainly for their oil. It was more valuable than the oil of other whales, burning very cleanly in lamps and candles, and making a good lubricant. Now they are protected. But how many are left? We do not know, but they are not rare or endangered. There are probably 300,000 to 400,000 altogether.

Where can we see them?

Blunt nose with a single nostril – it must be a sperm whale.

FEEDING

Sperm whales feed mainly on squid. Some they catch at the surface or in mid-water, but others they dive for, to great depths. They have a single row of peg-like teeth on either side of the lower jaw. They often feed at or below 3300 ft. (1000 m), and may go even deeper. Some of the squid are themselves enormous, even longer than the sperm whales. At depths below a few hundred meters the sea is permanently dark, so they cannot hunt by sight. Instead they probably use sonar – emitting series of clicks that bounce off the prey and show where it is. Sperm whales eat also both surface- and bottom-living fish.

The Azores have for centuries been centers of whale hunting. Each group of coastal villages had its whaleboat, with sail, oarsmen and harpooneer, and a lookout point on the cliff-tops. When whales – usually sperm whales – came within sight, the crews gathered from the farms and vineyards, launched the boats, and set off after them.

Sperm whales still feed within sight of the islands, but today it is whale watchers, rather than hunters, who go out to see them. In summer, between May and October, when the weather is calm, you can climb to the lookout points on the cliffs and see them passing, or take one of many launch trips from Horta or other centers.

Another good area for seeing sperm whales is the patch of deep water that lies off the northeast coast of New Zealand's South Island. The whales feed just a few kilometers off the town of Kaikoura, set wonderfully between high mountains and ocean. Most appear during the Southern Hemisphere winter months of May, June and July, but they are still there in summer, between November and March, when the weather is usually calmer. Summer is better too for seeing dusky dolphins, Hector's dolphins, and occasional beaked whales.

NEW ZEALAND

Kaikoura

THE CASE

The sperm whale's square-cut head contains a massive "case," or lump of waxy material called spermaceti. Nobody knows what it is for. It may be a kind of float, helping to keep the whale upright in the water, with its nostril high. The whale may be able to alter its density by cooling or warming it rapidly. That might alter the whale's total density, helping it to dive efficiently. It may act as a lens for sound, concentrating the whale's clicks into a narrow beam for echolocation. Perhaps it does all of these, and other things as well.

MINIATURE SPERM WHALES

Sperm whales share their family with two much smaller whales, pygmy sperm whales *(Kogia breviceps)* and dwarf sperm whales *(Kogia simus)*. These are small, like slow-moving dolphins, blue, gray or brown above and paler below, with rounded, rather shark-like heads and pointed lower jaws. Both have teeth in the lower jaw only, and a single nostril on the left side of the head. They do not look at all like sperm whales, but we think they are related because of the teeth, nostrils, shape of the skull, and rounded forehead containing spermaceti.

They are both species of warm and tropical seas, and not often seen. We know very little of their biology, but both are probably deep divers that bask only rarely at the surface. Pygmy sperm whales are 8.0–11.5 ft. (2.5–3.5 m) long and weigh up to 880 lbs. (400 kg). Dwarf sperm whales are smaller, seldom longer than 9 ft. (2.7 m) or heavier than 550 lbs. (250 kg).

Dwarf sperm whale

FACT FILE

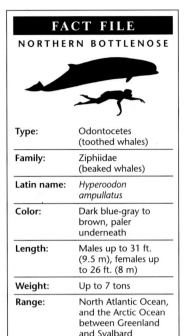

NORTHERN BOTTLENOSE

Type:	Odontocetes (toothed whales)
Family:	Ziphiidae (beaked whales)
Latin name:	*Hyperoodon ampullatus*
Color:	Dark blue-gray to brown, paler underneath
Length:	Males up to 31 ft. (9.5 m), females up to 26 ft. (8 m)
Weight:	Up to 7 tons
Range:	North Atlantic Ocean, and the Arctic Ocean between Greenland and Svalbard

SOUTHERN BOTTLENOSE

Type:	Odontocetes (toothed whales)
Family:	Balaenidae (right whales)
Latin name:	*Hyperoodon planifrons*
Color:	Dark gray-brown, paler underneath
Length:	Males probably up to 30 ft. (9 m), females slightly smaller
Weight:	Probably up to 7 tons
Range:	Antarctic Ocean and southern waters of Indian, Pacific and Atlantic oceans

IS IT A BOTTLENOSE?

Bottlenose whales are most often found in temperate or cold waters. Both kinds have been seen blowing among ice floes. Though they live far apart, the two species look very similar - medium-sized whales, slender and cylindrical like small submarines, with hooked dorsal fin set well back toward the tail and short, pointed flippers. Northern bottlenoses tend to be dark gray, southern bottlenoses often more brown, and both are paler underneath. Their faces too are pale, with beak-like mouth and rounded, bulging forehead, especially in large males.

BOTTLENOSE WHALES

Their faces reminded old-time sailors of squat, stubby wine bottles. Found only in deep water, usually far from land, bottlenose whales are dark, medium-sized whales that dive deep for food and tend to keep out of people's way.

THESE ARE MYSTERIOUS WHALES, members of a mysterious family that few people ever have a chance to see. The family, called the Ziphiidae, or beaked whales, includes 18 species of similar size, shape and color, all of which have small mouths with beak-like jaws. Some of the species are rare and have hardly ever been seen alive. We know them mainly from skulls and fragments of skeleton washed ashore.

Nearly all have only a few teeth, usually two or four, and only in the lower jaw. Some species have no teeth at all, though nearly all have vestiges (tiny teeth too small ever to appear) buried deep in their gums. In those that have them, the teeth are strange, unusual shapes, some pear-shaped, some flattened like blades, some long and narrow like tusks. Why the teeth of the bottlenose and beaked whales are so strangely varied, or how they use them, we do not know.

Male bottlenoses, both northern and southern, have two small, squat, pointed teeth, visible at the front of the lower jaw. In females the teeth are so small that they seldom appear at the surface. Old male bottlenoses often have long, narrow scars on their back. Perhaps they use their teeth more for fighting than for eating.

Northern bottlenoses are found as far south as the Canary Islands in winter, but seem to gather in colder waters during the summer. During the 19th century several thousand were taken by whalers for their oil.

Northern bottlenose whale.

Old male bottlenose

Adult female bottlenose

Difficult to spot

DIFFERENT KINDS

The two kinds of bottlenose whales, though very similar to each other, so far as we know keep well apart and never have a chance to meet. Northern bottlenoses appear in the North Atlantic Ocean, but not in the Pacific, and spread far north among the Arctic ice in summer. The southern species lives in all the southern oceans, penetrating far into the pack ice even in the depths of winter.

THE BEAKED WHALES

Here are the heads of some of the other kinds of beaked whales. Similar in size, shape and color, these whales show their greatest differences in the shapes and arrangement of their teeth. We do not know why these teeth are shaped as they are, or how the whales use them.

Stejnerger's beaked whale

Ginkgo-toothed whale

Blainville's beaked whale

Young bottlenose whale

The bottlenose whales, like others in the family of beaked whales, are among the most difficult cetaceans for whale watchers to see. They seldom swim close to the shore, and never in shallow waters, unless they are injured or ill. They live mainly in cool or cold waters, in areas where seas are often rough. Deep divers, they spend only a few minutes at a time on the surface. They seem to live alone or in small groups, seldom in large gatherings. Southern bottlenoses have always been rare. The northern species used to be more plentiful, but hunting during the 19th century reduced their numbers, and they are only now beginning to recover.

The most likely places for watchers to find them are off steep coasts, for example volcanic islands, where there is deep water close inshore. The Azores in the middle of the North Atlantic Ocean, rise steeply from the seabed, with deep channels between them. Northern bottlenose whales, together with other kinds of beaked whales, sperm whales and many surface-feeding species, visit regularly in summer. Whale-watching launches operate from Horta and other centers. Bottlenose and other kinds of beaked whale also can be seen off Iceland.

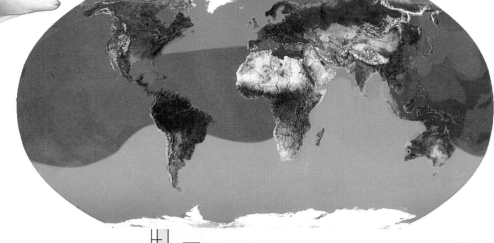

◻ SOUTHERN BOTTLENOSE

◼ NORTHERN BOTTLENOSE

FEEDING

Northern bottlenoses feed on shoaling fish, such as herrings, and several species of squid or cuttlefish, occasionally taking starfish as well. The small fish live in surface waters, and are probably easy to see, catch and swallow. The squid live several hundreds of feet below the surface, in a region too deep for sunlight to penetrate, and the starfish live even deeper, on the mud of the seabed. How do these whales catch their food? Many animals that live at great depths carry tiny lights, to attract food species toward themselves. Perhaps the whales see these lights and grab them. However, they probably use echolocation as well (p. 29), sending out streams of high-pitched sounds, which produce echoes that tell the whales where to find their prey.

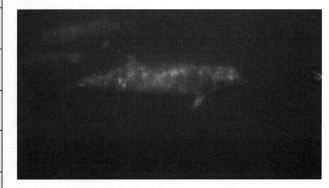

Dappled sunlight breaks the outline and helps to hide this bottlenose whale.

PILOT WHALES

So-called because they "pilot" or "lead" each other to shoals of fish, these are lively black dolphins that bustle around the oceans in huge groups - sometimes in dozens, sometimes in hundreds.

FACT FILE

LONG-FINNED PILOT WHALE

Type:	Odontocetes (toothed whales)
Family:	Delphinidae (dolphins)
Subfamily:	Orcinae
Latin name:	*Globicephala melas*
Color:	Dark blue-gray to black on top, white "anchor" underneath on throat, chest and abdomen; some with pale patches behind the dorsal fin and between the eyes
Length:	Males 15–20 ft. (4.5–6m), females up to 16 ft. (5 m)
Weight:	Males up to 4 tons, females to 2 tons
Range:	North Atlantic Ocean and Mediterranean Sea, also southern Atlantic, Indian and Pacific oceans

A RE THESE WHALES OR DOLPHINS? There is really no difference, except that we use "whale" for all the big cetaceans, and also for some of the lesser ones. Like killer whales (which are probably closely related), these are dolphins, but big ones - just big enough to be called whales.

Long-finned pilot whales swim fast, sometimes keeping up with moving ships, though not often riding the bow wave.

The calves, 3 feet (1 m) long at birth, are fed on milk for about 18 months. Though seldom if ever seen in the North Pacific Ocean, long-finned pilot whales are common in the North Atlantic and also in the southern oceans.

We do not know how many there are, but the total in both hemispheres is likely to run to tens or even hundreds of thousands.

They seem mostly to live well away from land and to feed mainly in deep water. Yet they are often washed up on beaches, sometimes dozens at a time, with dozens more darting about as though trying to leap ashore too. Perhaps their direction-finding sense - sound-based echolocation - works best in the open ocean, but becomes confused in shallows close to land.

Groups of pilot whales include males, females and calves. The females start to breed at six or seven years, and produce a calf about every third year.

IS IT A PILOT WHALE?

Long, black slinky dolphins, they usually swim in "schools" or groups numbering anything from a dozen to several hundred. Far bigger than most other dolphins, they have a large, prominent dorsal fin and backward-curving flippers with long, slender tips. The forehead bulges, and they have a curiously wide mouth with plenty of sharp white teeth, usually 7 to 12 on either side, top and bottom.

Groups whistle and click constantly. Because of their curious noises, northern fishermen know them as 'caa'ing' (calling) whales.

male

female

Where do we see pilot whales?

DISTRIBUTION

Long-finned pilot whales live only in temperate and cool seas. There are two quite separate populations - some biologists call them separate species, but individuals of the two are very similar. One lives in the North Atlantic Ocean, from northern Florida north to Newfoundland and Greenland, and across to Africa, western Europe and into the eastern Mediterranean Sea. The other population lives in cool latitudes of the South Atlantic, Indian and Pacific oceans.

Short-finned pilot whales live in the warm seas between, with some overlapping.

Long-finned pilot whale

Short-finned pilot whale

FEEDING

Pilot whales feed on squid, which they probably catch in deep water, and on fish, mostly schooling fish that they catch at the surface. Such big groups of whale-sized dolphins need a lot of food daily to keep them going. A school of fifty would need to catch at least 3300 lbs. (1500 kg) of fish every day.

Whale watchers are likely to see pilot whales wherever there are rich patches of sea. Often you see them incidentally to other species. You will seldom see one on its own. Where there is one, there are usually at least a dozen, then another group just like them not far away, and then probably another. Often they move in loose, shifting groups of hundreds.

It is easy to tell when pilot whales are about. The sea seems suddenly full of black dorsal fins. If the whales are feeding on fish shoals, there will usually be swarms of seabirds over them, ready to pick up the scraps. Though sociable among themselves, these whales show little interest in boats, and need to be approached carefully.

In the Atlantic Ocean long-finned pilot whales occur off Iceland, the Faroes, the Orkney and Shetland islands, mainland Scotland and Ireland, and Norway. They are found occasionally off Newfoundland (where they were formerly hunted) and often off New England. In the Southern Hemisphere you see them off Tasmania, southern Australia, and New Zealand, around the Falkland Islands, and off the southern coast of South Africa.

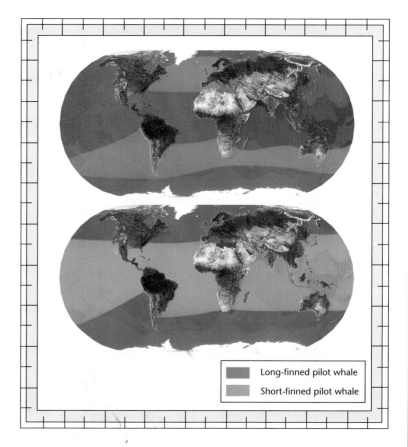

Long-finned pilot whale
Short-finned pilot whale

Short-finned pilot whales (see below), their tropical equivalent, can be visited in the Canary Islands (there are daily whale-watching cruises from ports on Tenerife) and the Azores. Sometimes they appear in the Caribbean and around the Galápagos Islands, throughout Malasia, off southern Japan and around Hawaii.

LONG-FINNED AND SHORT-FINNED PILOT WHALES

Long-finned pilot whales are very seldom seen in equatorial waters. So there seems to be a wide gap between the two populations, making it unlikely that those of the Northern Hemisphere ever meet those of the south. Yet individuals of the two populations are very similar in appearance, size and every other respect. The equatorial gap is filled by a very similar but different species, the short-finned pilot whale (*Globicephala macrorhynchus*). These have notably shorter fins, though still with the swept-back, pointed look, and they also have fewer teeth. However, short-finned pilot whales live almost entirely in tropical and equatorial waters, including the northern Pacific Ocean, overlapping only slightly with their long-finned cousins.

DOLPHIN OR PORPOISE?

All the smaller members of the Odontocetes, or toothed whales, are called either dolphins or porpoises. What is a dolphin, what is a porpoise, and what are the differences between them? Biologists divide all the living toothed whales into seven families, all with long names.

We have already met members of three of these families:
■ the Ziphiidae (beaked and bottlenose whales, pp. 30–31).
■ the Physeteridae (sperm whales, pp. 28–29).
■ the Monodontidae (narwhals and belugas, pp. 24–25).

That leaves just four families, which include all the different kinds of dolphins and porpoises.

Three of the families include dolphins:
■ the Platanistidae (four species of river dolphins).
■ the Stenidae (four species of long-beaked dolphins).
■ the Delphinidae (27 species of "true" dolphins). Some of these are shown on these two pages. Note that we have already met some of the Delphinidae: killer whales (pp 26–27) and pilot whales (p. 32–33) are both really dolphins, but called whales because they are big.

The fourth family:
■ the Phocoenidae (six species of porpoises) is dealt with on the next two pages.

DOLPHINS

These are some of the smaller cetaceans. Lively, inquisitive, playful, often noisy, always active, they live in large family groups and are plentiful in all but the coldest oceans. They include the most colorful of all the cetaceans.

THE THREE DOLPHIN families together include 35 species. Typical dolphins have a long beak with rows of sharp teeth, and a rounded "forehead" with twin nostrils. Apart from the big killer and pilot whales, they are all within the range 5–10 feet (1.5–3 m) long, sleek, fast-moving, usually dark above and paler below, and patterned with stripes or spots.

There are four species each of river dolphins and long-beaked dolphins. The rest are so-called true dolphins - really a mixed group for which nobody has thought of a better name. There are so many of these that biologists divide them into subfamilies, according to different characteristics. For example, the pilot and killer whales, which are thought to be closely related, are included in the subfamily Orcinae, and the 15 species most closely related to common dolphins form the subfamily Delphinidae.

Spinner dolphin

Atlantic spotted dolphin

Rough-toothed dolphin

Bottlenose dolphin

Common dolphin

Dusky dolphin

Risso's dolphin

Amazon river dolphin

Striped dolphin

Where do we see dolphins?

Marine park ranger at Shark Bay, Western Australia, with friendly bottlenose dolphins.

Clymene dolphin

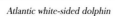

Commerson's dolphin

Atlantic white-sided dolphin

White-beaked dolphin

Hourglass dolphin

Dolphins occur in all the oceans, except for the coldest waters of the Arctic and Antarctic oceans. They move in groups, so must live where there is food enough for all - often among islands, in places where currents meet, or areas of upwelling where waters rich in nutrients are drawn up from the seabed. There are plenty of dolphins in cool waters. Around Britain, especially off Wales, Devon and Cornwall, look out for bottlenose, white-beaked and common dolphins. New England, the St. Lawrence estuary and Iceland have white-beaked and Atlantic white-sided dolphins. Japan and Alaska offer Pacific white-sided and bottlenose dolphins.

Off Patagonia and the Falkland Islands look for Commerson's, Peale's, dusky and rare hourglass dolphins. New Zealand offers, among several other species, Hector's,

bottlenose, Risso's and dusky dolphins. However, you see more kinds of dolphins in warmer tropical and subtropical waters. Near Gibraltar you may see common, striped and bottlenose dolphins. Around the Canaries, Azores, Bermuda and Caribbean islands, and off the Brazilian coast, look for spinners, spotted and rough-toothed dolphins. Southern Japan has bottlenose, striped and common dolphins. Hawaii provides a wide range, including rough-toothed,

striped, bridled, spinner and bottlenose dolphins. The four kinds of river dolphins are each confined to one river system; Indian river dolphins to the Indus, Ganges and Brahmaputra rivers; Amazon dolphins to the Amazon and neighboring coastal seas, Negro and Maramon rivers; white-fin dolphins to the Yangtse; and La Plata dolphins to the La Plata estuary and neighboring South American seas. All live in muddy water, and are difficult to spot from ships unless you are really looking for them.

Common dolphins following a boat off Eigg, West Scotland.

A SELECTION OF DOLPHINS

Rough-toothed dolphin (*Steno bredanensis*). Tropical and warm temperate oceanic waters.

Common dolphin (*Delphinus delphis*). Widespread in temperate and tropical seas.

Risso's dolphin (*Grampus griseus*). Temperate and tropical seas throughout the world, usually offshore.

Spinner dolphin (*Stenella longirostris*). Worldwide in tropics: oceanic, found offshore in deep waters.

Atlantic spotted dolphin (*Stenella plagiodon*). Tropical and warm temperate Atlantic and Caribbean waters.

Bottlenose dolphin (*Tursiops truncatus*). Temperate and tropical oceans worldwide: often close inshore.

Striped dolphin (*Stenella coeruleoalba*). Wide distribution in tropical and temperate oceanic waters.

Clymene dolphin (*Stenella clymene*). Warm temperate and tropical Atlantic waters.

Hourglass dolphin (*Lagenorhynchus cruciger*). Cold waters of the southern oceans.

Commerson's dolphin (*Cephalorhynchus commersonii*). Restricted to southern South America and the Falkland Islands.

Atlantic white-sided dolphin (*Lagenorhynchus acutus*). Temperate and cold North Atlantic Ocean and Norwegian sea.

White-beaked dolphin (*Lagenorhynchus albirostris*). A cold-water species of the North Atlantic Ocean and Norwegian Sea.

Amazon river dolphin (*Inia geoffrensis*). Amazon river system and neighboring coasts of South America.

Dusky dolphin (*Lagenorhynchus obscurus*). Cool temperate southern waters off New Zealand, Patagonia and southern South Africa.

Left: Bottlenose dolphin, showing the typical peg-like teeth.

PORPOISES

Some people call any very small cetacean a "porpoise," especially if it has a rounded face without much of a beak. Most biologists think that the six species described on these pages - and only these - should be called porpoises. They are sufficiently alike to form a natural family, called the Phocoenidae [foe-seen-ih-day]. Other small, round-faced cetaceans may look like porpoises, but have other characters that link them more firmly to one or other of the dolphin families.

Dall's porpoises approaching the surface.

Porpoises include some of the smallest of all the cetaceans. They are generally short and chubby, with rounded faces and no distinct beak. Their teeth are flattened or spade-shaped rather than pointed. Usually they have about 23 on either side, up and down. The dorsal fin is triangular, never tilted backward. One kind has no dorsal fin at all. Like dolphins, they live in groups or schools. Many live in shallow water, so we see them quite often in harbors and bays. Sadly, many are caught and killed accidentally each year in fishing nets.

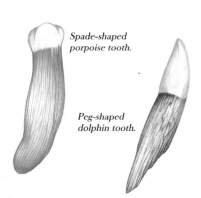

Spade-shaped porpoise tooth.

Peg-shaped dolphin tooth.

PORPOISES

Sometimes called "the mice of the ocean," they are the smallest of all the cetaceans. Schools of porpoises often follow boats, and appear in harbors and bays close inshore.

THOUGH SIMILAR IN SHAPE and color to dolphins, and often mistaken for them, porpoises are usually shorter, fatter, and less colorful. Their faces are rounder, without any kind of beak. Most are black or dark brownish gray above, white or pale to dark gray below, and they lack the colorful stripes and splashes that brighten so many of the dolphins.

Only one species, the common porpoise, is widespread, though only in the Northern Hemisphere. Its other name, "harbour porpoise," is given because it sometimes follows boats into harbors. It feeds mainly on fish. Dall's porpoise, another northern species, lives only in cooler waters of the North Pacific Ocean, hunting squid and fish. William Dall, a 19th-century seaman and explorer, collected the first-ever specimen off Alaska.

The third northern species, the Californian porpoise, is restricted entirely to the Gulf of California. Popularly called *cochito* (Spanish for "little pig"), or *vaquita* ("little cow"), it feeds mainly on fish and shrimps.

The finless porpoise has a wide range from the Gulf of Aden to China and southern Japan. It hunts for fish and shrimps in muddy estuaries and swamps. Spectacled porpoises and Burmeister's porpoises are both restricted to cool South American waters, where they hunt fish and squid. Why spectacled? Because they have a dark ring round each eye. Who was Burmeister? A 19th-century German biologist working in Argentina who described the first-known specimen.

Spectacled porpoise

Californian porpoise

Where do we find porpoises?

Harbor porpoise caught and drowned in a fishing net.

Dall's porpoise

Whale watchers usually see porpoises as a bonus, while they are out at sea watching for bigger species.

■ Common porpoises may turn up anywhere from Japan to California, from New England to North Africa, in the Mediterranean and Black seas. You can watch them from harbor walls or cliff-tops, or from small offshore fishing boats. Larger boats often scare them away. The best conditions are calm or slightly ruffled water. They are too small to spot in rough or even choppy seas. If they are fishing, they will stay for some minutes. If not, they move on quickly.

■ Dall's porpoise can similarly be seen in the North Pacific Ocean, from the Bering Strait to Japan and California. Look out for them especially off Alaska, Vancouver Island and Japan. Not at all shy, they often gather around boats, and enjoy riding the bow waves. They are quite unmistakable - dark blue-black on top, dazzling white

underneath, with a fashionable white flash on the dorsal fin.

■ Californian porpoises or cochitos, smallest of all the porpoises, are rare and not easily seen. You may be lucky enough to spot one or two on whale-watching trips in the Gulf of California.

■ Finless porpoises are widespread in their tropical home waters, though nowhere especially numerous or concentrated. Why have they no dorsal fin? We do not know, but calves are said to ride on their mother's back, in the place where the dorsal fin should be.

Harbor porpoise.

The two species of South American porpoises are among the most difficult of all for whale watchers to see.

■ Spectacled porpoises, which are the largest of the family, live quietly in the deep fjords of Tierra del Fuego, along the coast of Patagonia, and in the channels and waterways of the Falkland Islands. Dead ones have been found on beaches of southern islands in the Indian and Pacific oceans. A few are caught each year in Argentine fishermen's nets. Elsewhere, even in the Falkland Islands, very few people have had the chance to see them, alive or dead.

■ Burmeister's porpoises too are shy and hard to spot. Chilean fishermen sometimes see them or catch them in nets off the west coast of South America, and dead ones are from time to time washed up on the beaches. They move in small groups and tend to keep away from boats.

THE FAMILY OF PORPOISES

Common (harbor) porpoise (*Phocoena phocoena*). Wide distribution in the Northern Hemisphere from Arctic to subtropical waters.

Californian porpoise (*Phocoena sinus*). Found only in the Gulf of California, mainly at its northern end.

Spectacled porpoise (*Phocoena dioptrica*). East coast of South America from La Plata estuary to Tierra del Fuego, Falkland Islands and South Georgia.

Finless porpoise (*Neophocoena phocaenoides*). Coastal waters of southern and eastern Asia from the Persian Gulf to Malaysia, China and Japan.

Burmeister's porpoise (*Phocoena spinipennis*). South America from La Plata estuary to Tierra del Fuego, along the west coast to northern Peru.

Dall's porpoise (*Phocoenoides dalli*). North Pacific Ocean, from Bering Strait to Japan and California.

Burmeister's porpoise

Finless porpoise

Common (harbour) porpoise

CETACEANS ASHORE

Whales and dolphins sometimes come ashore alive. Often it is only one, but occasionally whole schools or groups come ashore, as many as two or three dozen at a time. What can we do to help them?

If you see a dead whale or dolphin lying on the shore, telephone the nearest museum, university or college biology department, a public library, or a police station. One or other should be able to put you in touch with a whale scientist who would be interested, and the police will want to know so they can report the stranding to the public health authorities.

If you have a camera, take several photographs of the body from different angles. If you have pencil and paper, draw sketches of it. Measure it as accurately as you can. From this information, somebody may be able to identify it. Ring the newsdesk of the local newspaper. They may send a reporter to write a story about it, and perhaps a photographer to take a picture.

Some species of whales and dolphins are known only from their skulls, or from badly damaged remains, so a freshly dead specimen may be very valuable to scientists. In New Zealand a few years ago a farmer telephoned the local university to report a dead whale, washed up on a remote beach. It turned out to belong to a very rare species, Shephard's beaked whale, that was previously known only from a skull and incomplete fragments of a skeleton. Nobody had ever before seen the whole whale. Thanks to that farmer, the scientists were able to measure and photograph it, examine it fully and eventually collect its complete skeleton.

MANY WHALES AND DOLPHINS die at sea, where their bodies break up and are eaten by fish and other scavengers. Most of these we never see and know nothing about.

Sometimes cetaceans that have recently died float to the surface, drift with winds and currents and are eventually washed ashore. If they have been dead for several days they may look terrible and smell even worse. People usually want to get rid of them, by burying them in the sand or pushing them back out to sea as soon as possible.

However, a dead whale may be very interesting to scientists, who do not mind the smell. Some dead whales may be calves or young animals that are seldom seen, alive or dead. Some may be very rare or even unknown species. Scientists who are interested in whales may want to photograph and measure a dead specimen, cut it up to find out why it died, or collect its skull or skeleton.

Left: Sperm whale stranded on a beach in Scotland.

What to do for a stranded whale

Some whales that are obviously injured, sick or weak may have drifted into shallow water and been grounded by a falling tide. Others seem fit and healthy but quite unable to return to sea once they are stranded. Either way they need help, and you may be able to do something for them.

If you see a stranded whale or dolphin, try to see first if it is still alive. The eyes, jaws, flippers or tail may be moving. It may be breathing, though sometimes only a single breath every few minutes. Watch the blowhole and chest wall for movement. You may see the heart beating against the chest wall. If the whale is alive, here's what you can do.

■ Try to get help. Phone the police and ask them to get in touch with the nearest whale experts. In some places where whales come ashore often, there are local groups of people already organized who know just how to help.

■ Keep away from the tail, which may suddenly lash out and knock you over.

■ Keep the skin cool and moist. You can do this by shading it from the sun, sprinkling water or damp sand over the flippers, head and back, or covering it with damp cloths. If the mouth is open, keep the inside damp with an occasional spray of water.

■ Be careful to keep the blowhole free of water or sand, and do not cover it with cloth. Remember that a whale cannot breathe through its mouth.

■ Move quietly and ask other people to stay quiet. If there are people standing around, get them to bring water and covering, or use their mobile phones to bring help.

■ If it is a small porpoise or dolphin, you may be able to carry it back to the sea. Do not tug at the flippers, tail or skin, as they are easily damaged. Try to roll it onto a stretcher or strong sacking, and get several people to lift it that way.

■ If it is too heavy to carry, you may have to wait a few hours until the next tide comes in. Once the water has taken its weight, a few strong helpers may be able to turn it and push it out to sea.

■ Do not be surprised - or sad - if a cetacean dies while you are trying to help. It is not your fault. There was probably something seriously wrong, and it would have died anyway. However, if you can help a cetacean back to the sea, you will probably remember it for the rest of your life.

Caring for a young minke whale in northern Australia.

Left: Long-finned pilot whales washed up among backbones of long-dead rorquals

HOW CAN WE HELP?

How can we help to protect whales, porpoises and dolphins?

The best way is to join one of the groups and societies that are interested in saving cetaceans. Almost every country has one or several such societies. Write to them for information about what they do. If you can help them, or they can help you, see about joining them.

They will probably send information about where to see whales or who to contact. Some have "adopt-a-dolphin" schemes: for a few dollars you can "adopt" a particular dolphin in the wild – even go out to visit it. They may also send you lists of books, videos, posters and other information to buy or borrow.

Here are some addresses:

Marine Mammal Fund
Fort Mason Center
Building E
San Francisco, CA 94123
(Tel: 415-775-4636)

Save the Whales
1426 Main Street
P.O. Box 2397
Venice, CA 90291
(Tel: 310-392-6226)

American Cetacean Society
P.O. Box 1391
San Pedro, CA 90733-1391
(http://www.acsonline.org)

Marine Mammal Stranding Center
Box 773
Brigantine, NJ 08203
(http://www.mmsc.org)

Other contact addresses can be found on page 48.

This Scottish beach is the last resting place of many stranded whales.

WHALE HUNTING

For thousands of years people have hunted cetaceans, mainly for meat and fat. The earliest whalers, hundreds of years ago, could only drive whales ashore. Later they learned to sail or row up alongside them and catch them with nets or long spears. It was dangerous hunting but worth while. A whale or a few dolphins could provide a whole village with meat and oil to last the winter.

CETACEANS & MAN

Man has always hunted whales, dolphins and porpoises. Today there is less need to kill them - we can watch them and enjoy them alive instead.

Cutting up a fin whale at a whaling station.

In medieval times hunters went after the whales in ships, first close to home, then in more distant waters, even as far away as the Arctic. The harpooned whales were towed to the side of the ship and stripped of baleen ("whalebone") and blubber. The baleen was dried and used to make brushes and other useful things. The blubber was boiled down to make oil, which was burned in lamps to light homes and city streets. In the 18th and 19th centuries deepsea whaling employed hundreds of ships and thousands of men.

PRIMITIVE COAST-DWELLING PEOPLE killed just enough cetaceans to feed their small families and settlements, leaving plenty more in the sea. Commercial whalers took far more, selling the baleen and oil all over the world. Soon the hunters were killing whales faster than the whales could breed, and some species - right, gray and sperm whales, for example - became very scarce.

Fast, steam-driven catchers with explosive harpoons made it possible to attack and kill every kind of whale. During the first half of the 20th century the big rorquals became the main targets of a very efficient industry. They too became scarce.

The big whales were saved when farmers and foresters planted huge areas of the tropics with palms and other oil-bearing shrubs and trees. These yielded vegetable oils that were easier and cheaper to produce than whale oil.

Commercial whaling declined, and now has almost ceased. Native peoples of the Arctic still take a few whales each year for food. Only the Norwegians and Japanese continue to hunt commercially, mainly because they like to eat whale meat.

Still, thousands of dolphins and porpoises are hunted every year for food, and even more are killed accidentally by being caught in fishing nets.

Scientists firing a radio tag at a gray whale. The tag will transmit signals that can be picked up ashore, telling the scientists of the whale's day-to-day movements.

Cetaceans at risk

COMMERCIAL WHALING

In the 19th century whalers invented a harpoon with an explosive head that could be fired from a cannon on the bow of a fast steamship. Now they could tackle any whale, no matter how large or fast. During the early 20th century thousands of whales were killed and processed in floating factories that could haul the carcasses aboard, cut them up and turn them into oil, animal feed and fertilizers. Oil was no longer used for lighting, but for food, soap and other household products. So great was the demand that, by the mid-century, stocks of all the big whales were severely reduced.

Today there is very little commercial whaling, and what remains is carefully watched by the International Whaling Commission. Many people are thankful that whaling has almost finished, and will not want to see it start again when whales become more plentiful.

Though whale hunting has almost ceased, many thousands of dolphins and porpoises are killed each year for food. These are taken mainly by people in countries where other kinds of meat are rare or expensive.

Sadly, many whales and tens of thousands of dolphins and porpoises die accidentally each year by drowning in fishermen's nets. Most of them are caught in drift nets - huge nets, up to 25 miles (40 km) long, that hang in the sea like curtains. Shoals of surface-feeding fish drift into the nets, followed by tuna, swordfish, albacore and other large and valuable fish, which are what the fishermen are hoping to catch.

However, whales, dolphins and porpoises also follow the fish and become entangled. Once they are caught, they are almost certain to drown.

Wherever big nets of this kind are used, they catch seals and cetaceans as well.

Yearly catches of small cetaceans include:
■ 3000- 4000 harbor porpoises of Newfoundland, and up to 2000 in the Gulf of St. Lawrence
■ 5000-10,000 striped dolphins in the Mediterranean Sea
■ over 7000 Dall's porpoises in the North Pacific Ocean
■ over 1300 Risso's dolphins and 4000 spinner dolphins off Sri Lanka
■ over 1700 bottlenose dolphins off Australia.

The problem is that cetateans cannot see these fine nets, or detect them by echo-location. Big whales probably blunder into them. Dolphins and porpoises chasing fish do not realize they are there until it is too late.

Left: In many parts of the world, whale watching has replaced whale hunting completely.

Divers swimming with bottlenose dolphins in the Red Sea.

One way of saving cetaceans from this danger is for fishermen to hang metal or plastic balls on the nets, to make them easier to see. However, they need to hang a lot of these "reflectors" to make it worthwhile. Fishermen dislike using them because they are expensive, and make it harder to handle the very big nets and bring them back on board.

Another way is for governments to stop fishermen from using big drift nets, especially in places where they are a danger to rare dolphins or porpoises. This too is not always easy. Fishermen say that big nets are the only practical way to catch the fish, and banning the nets means that they can no longer earn a living.

Bottlenose dolphin taking a friendly interest.

WHAT CAN WE DO?

The best way to save whales, dolphins and porpoises is to get as many people as possible interested in them. Throughout the United States and many European countries there are clubs and societies of people who love these wonderful animals. They want to see them, read about them, and help them to

live freely. Why not join them? You will find some addresses on page 39 and more on p.48

Gray whale entangled in fishing nets. Many thousands of whales, dolphins and porpoises die each year by being caught in big nets set for fish.

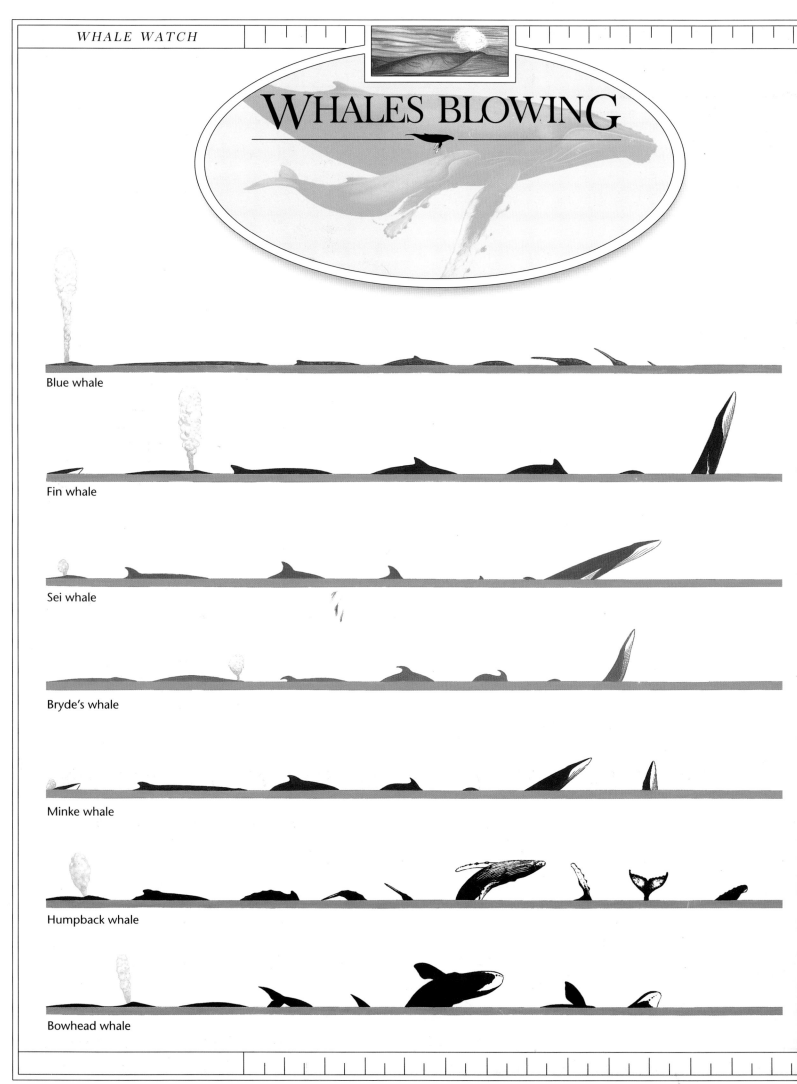

WHALES BLOWING

Blue whale

Fin whale

Sei whale

Bryde's whale

Minke whale

Humpback whale

Bowhead whale

Grey whale

Killer whale

Here are diagrams of cetaceans at the surface. In each case the animal is moving from left to right. First the top of the head appears, then a "blow," or spout, then the back (with dorsal fin), then the tail, which often stands clear out of the water, especially when the whale is about to make a deep dive. Sometimes they stick their head out of the water, falling back in with a big splash.

Gray whale

Northern and southern right whale

Sperm whale

Killer whale

Dolphin

Porpoise

DIFFERENT SPECIES, DIFFERENT SPOUTS

Experienced whale watchers can sometimes identify a whale from its spout alone. Here are some typical spouts, drawn roughly to scale.

Humpback

Right

Blue

Fin

Sei

Minke

Gray

Sperm

GLOSSARY

Can you identify these species - answers below

Top: Dusky dolphin.
Middle: Minke whale.
Bottom: Pilot whale.

aquatic	Living in the sea or freshwater.
baleen	Sheets of horny material in the mouths of mysticete ("whalebone") whales, with frayed edges that filter food from seawater.
barnacle	Crab-like animal that lives in a chalky shell attached to rocks or driftwood; some attach themselves to whales.
blowhole	Cetacean's nostril, usually found on top of the head, through which the animal breathes.
blubber	Layer of fat under the skin of whales, seals and other marine animals.
bow wave	Wave produced by the bow (front) of a boat moving through water.
canyon	Deep valley.
Cetacea	Natural group of warm-blooded aquatic animals comprising the whales, dolphins and porpoises.
Crustacea	Natural group of animals with a hard shell and jointed limbs, which includes crabs. lobsters, shrimps and prawns.
diatom	Tiny plant that lives in millions at the ocean surface, foming part of the phytoplankton (see plankton).
dolphin	Small cetacean belonging to the families Platinistidae, Stenidae or Delphinidae, usually with pointed face and rounded forehead and pointed teeth.
dorsal fin	Small, single fin on the back of most cetaceans.
echo-location	See sonar.
endotherm	Animal (e.g., bird or mammal) that can maintain a high and constant body temperature; warm-blooded.
flipper	Flattened forelimb (equivalent to arm and hand) of whale, seal or penguin, used in swimming.
flukes	Flat lobes on either side of a cetacean's tail.
harpoon	Spear for killing whales.
hemisphere	Half the world.
lagoon	Lake close to the shore.

migration	Yearly or seasonal movement of animals from one part of the world to another.
Mysticetes	Group of whales that have no teeth, but feed by filtering food from the sea using baleen.
nitrogen	Gas, forming about four-fifths of the air we breathe; taken in by the body but not used.
oceanarium	Large pool where whales, porpoises and dophins are kept in captivity.
Odontocetes	Group of cetaceans that have teeth at some time in their lives, including some whales and all the porpoises and dolphins.
oxygen	Gas, forming about one-fifth of the air we breathe, that helps to keep us alive.
plankton	Tiny plants (phytoplankton) and animals (zooplankton) that float in surface waters of seas and lakes, often eaten by larger animals.
porpoise	Small cetacean belonging to the family Phocoenidae, with rounded face and head and flat, spade-like teeth.
pregnant	Carrying a developing baby inside the body.
prey	Animal that is hunted and killed by others.
pygmy	Very small.
rorqual	One of five kinds of mysticete whales, slender, fast-swimming.
sonar	Way of detecting objects at a distance by transmitting high-pitched sounds and receiving echoes; the time taken for the echo to come back is a measure of distance.
stock	Population or natural group of animals.
submarine bank	Hill under the sea.
volcanic islands	Islands formed from lava or ash thrown up by volcanoes.
waterlogged	Soaked with water.
whale	Large cetacean.
whalebone	See baleen.
whaling station	Factory where whales are cut up and turned into oil, meat and bone meal.

Top: Humpback whale.
Middle: Gray whale.
Bottom: Male killer whale.

INDEX

B
baleen 11, 15, 16, 17, 20, 21, 22, 40
barnacles 16, 23
Bering Strait 9
blowing 10, 42-43
blubber 13, 40
breathing 10

C
California 9
calving 22
cetaceans, and man 40-41
   ashore 38-39
   at risk 41
   basic kinds 11
   saving 41

D
diving 12-13
dolphins 34-35
   Amazon river 34, 35
   Atlantic spotted 34, 35
   black 12
   bottlenose 35
     swimming with divers 41
   catches, yearly 41
   Clymene 35
   Commerson's 35
   common 10, 34-35
   dusky 29, 34, 35
   Hector's 10, 29, 35
   hourglass 35
   Indian river 35
   killer whale, See whales
   Peale's 35
   pilot whales, See whales
   Risso's 34, 35
   rough-toothed 34, 35
   spinner 34, 35
   striped 34, 35
   tooth of 36
   white-beaked 35

E
echo-location 31 (see also sonar)
evolution of cetaceans 11

F
feeding 15, 17, 18, 20, 21, 22, 27, 29, 31, 33

G
Gerlache Strait, Antarctica 9
Gloucester, Mass. 9

H
Hawaii 9
Hermanus, South Africa 9
Horta, Azores 9

I
International Whaling
Commission 41

K
Kaikoura, New Zealand 9
keeping warm 12, 13

L
length, comparative 10, 11
lice, on gray whales 23

M
migration 22, 23, 25

O
Oban, Scotland 9
oceans, trailing whales across 9

P
porpoises 34, 36-37, 43
   Burmeister's 36, 37
   Californian 36, 37
   catches, yearly 41
   common (harbor) 36, 37
   Dall's 36, 37
   finless 37
   harbor, See porpoises,
   common
   spectacled 36, 37
   tooth of 36

S
Shikoku, Japan 9
size, comparative 10, 11
skin 13
sonar 29 (see also echo-location)
sounding 14
spermaceti 29
spouting 19
swimming 12, 13

T
tails 11, 14
teeth 11, 25, 29, 30, 31, 35, 36
temperature, body 8
Tenerife, Canary Is 9
toothed whales 34

U
Unicorns 24

V
Vancouver Island 9

W
whale watching 8-9, 40-41
whalebone 11
whales 14-33
   ancestors of 11
   at home 12-13
   beaked 29, 30-31
   belugas, 12, 24-25
   Blainville's beaked 31
   blowing 42-43
   blue 10-11, 18-19, 42, 43
   bottlenose 10, 12, 30-31
   bowhead 16-17, 42
    Alaskan 17
   Bryde's 20-21, 42
   fin 20-21, 42, 43
   gingo-toothed 31
   gray 22-23
    blowing 43
    entangled 41
    migration of 23
    tagged 40
   humpback 10-11, 13, 14-15, 42, 43
    tail prints of 14
   killer 26-27, 43
    in captivity 27
   minke 20-21, 42, 43
    stranded 39
   narwhals 10, 24-25
   pilot 32-33
   right 16-17, 43
    black 16, 17
    Greenland 16, 17
    pygmy 17
    southern 17
   rorquals 18, 20-21
   sei 20-21, 42, 43
   Shephard's beaked 38
   sperm 10-11, 12, 28-29, 43
    dwarf 29
    pygmy 29
    stranded 38
   Stejnerger's beaked 31
   stranded 12, 38-39
whaling 29, 40-41
   in the 19th century 41

HOW CAN YOU HELP?

If you are interested in whales, dolphins or porpoises there are many clubs and societies throughout America and Europe. Here are just a few.

Marine Mammal Fund
Fort Mason Center
Building E
San Francisco, CA 94123
415-775-4636

Save the Whales
1426 Main Street
P.O. Box 2397
Venice, CA 90291
310-392-6226

American Cetacean Society
P.O. Box 2639
San Pedro, CA 90731
310-548-6279

American Oceans Campaign
725 Arizona Ave
Suite 102
Santa Monica
CA 90401
800-862-3260
310-576-6162

Earth Island Institute
Save the Dolphin Project
300 Broadway
Suite 28
San Francisco, CA 94133
800-Dolphin
415-788-3666

Britain
Whale and Dolphin
Conservation Society
Alexander House
Janus Street West
Bath BA1 2BT
United Kingdom